Keeping Your Child in Mind

Overcoming Defiance, Tantrums, and
Other Everyday Behavior Problems by
Seeing the World Through Your Child's Eyes

Claudia M. Gold, MD

A MERLOYD LAWRENCE BOOK
LIFELONG BOOKS • DA CAPO PRESS
A Member of the Perseus Books Group

Copyright © 2011 by Claudia M. Gold, MD

Designed by Pauline Brown
Set in 12 point Goudy Oldstyle Std by the Perseus Books Group

Gold, Claudia M.
    Keeping your child in mind : overcoming defiance, tantrums, and other everyday behavior problems by seeing the world through your child's eyes / Claudia M. Gold.—1st Da Capo Press ed.
        p.   cm.
    "A Merloyd Lawrence Book."
    Includes bibliographical references.
    ISBN 978-0-7382-1485-6 (alk. paper)
    ISBN 978-07382-1529-7 (e-book)
    1. Problem children. 2. Behavior disorders in children. 3. Parenting. 4. Child rearing. I. Title.
    HQ773.G646   2011
    649'.64—dc22
                                                                        2011012655

First Da Capo Press edition 2011
Published as a Merloyd Lawrence book, by Da Capo Press
A Member of the Perseus Books Group
www.dacapopress.com

Da Capo Press books are available at special discounts for bulk purchases in the U.S. by corporations, institutions, and other organizations. For more information, please contact the Special Markets Department at the Perseus Books Group, 2300 Chestnut Street, Suite 200, Philadelphia, PA 19103, or call (800) 810-4145, ext. 5000, or e-mail special.markets@perseusbooks.com.

10 9 8 7 6 5 4 3 2 1

For Joe, Suzanne,
Hannah, and Eli

CONTENTS

ACKNOWLEDGMENTS

I would like to thank the following people for their critical role in bringing this book into existence:

My agent, Lisa Adams, who, with her kind and gentle manner, firmly and brilliantly led my book in the right direction

My editor, Merloyd Lawrence, who always understood exactly what I was trying to say, and with her magnificent editing helped me to say it ever more clearly

Peter Fonagy, Linda Mayes, David Reiss, and Arietta Slade, who offered inspiration as well as generous guidance and encouragement

Don MacGillis, editor at the *Boston Globe*, who first published my work and was instrumental in building my "platform"

Gale Pryor, great friend, high school classmate, and freelance editor, who believed in my project from the start

M. Gerard Fromm, Winnicott scholar, who taught me the true meaning of the phrase "the holding environment"

My parents, Henry and Edith Meininger, who shared with me a passion for writing and for caring for children

My husband, Joe, who works hard to earn a living so I can pursue these passions, and who always makes me laugh

And last but not least, my children, who are not only my greatest joy, but also my greatest teachers.

"IT'S NOT ABOUT THE SOUP": HOLDING YOUR CHILD IN MIND

aniel's mother Karen left a desperate message on the voice mail at my behavioral pediatrics practice. "There must be something wrong with him. You need to tell me what to do to make him listen!" The three of us met in my office two days later. The story of a terrible scene burst out of Karen, a painful drama that ended with five-year-old Daniel alone in his room refusing dinner after two hours of nonstop screaming. "What I want to hear from both of you is how you got to this point," I said. Karen was agitated, and in the face of his mother's anger, Daniel withdrew into his play, but as I worked with them to slow things down, the following story emerged. Daniel and his mother took turns telling the story from their own points of view.

It began after five o'clock on a day that Karen had been gone at her new job. Three months earlier, she had returned to work full time. Daniel, his mother, and his two-year-old sister Hailey had had a nice outing to the grocery store to shop for dinner. They had all agreed that they wanted hamburgers. Because the kids had been so well behaved, Karen offered to go to the store to get a special toy for Daniel to replace one that had recently broken. In his excitement, Daniel ran ahead in the parking lot. It was dark and Karen yelled to him to stay close, which he did. Unfortunately the store did not have the toy they were looking for, but Karen agreed to try a different store. They never made it to the second store. Once again, Daniel ran ahead, but this time he did not respond to his mother's call. Karen had to scream at him to stop running. "Mom was worried about you," I said. "It was dark and you could have been hurt." When they finally were back in the car and buckled in, Karen, feeling exhausted and overwhelmed, said she was not going to another store. Daniel then hit Hailey, who started to cry. I asked Daniel how he had felt at that moment. He was very clear. "I was sad." "Were you angry?" I asked. He looked at his mother. "Was I angry?" I said I wanted to know from him. "No," he said. "I was sad."

What had happened next didn't make sense. Karen felt at the end of her rope. Daniel and Hailey were both crying. Then

Daniel had said, "I want soup." This statement had the unfortunate effect of taking the conflict to a whole new level. Daniel and his mother went head-to-head over the dinner choice, and the battle continued for the next two hours, ending with Karen still in a rage and Daniel alone in his room without dinner. "Why," I wondered aloud with them in my office, "would Daniel take a situation that was already pretty bad, and then make it so much worse?" None of us knew the answer. "I wonder," I said, "if the soup was Daniel's way of saying, 'I feel bad and I need to be comforted.'" I told them that I had this idea because Daniel had told us that he felt sad, not angry.

With this suggestion the conversation took a new direction, as Karen began to tell me about an episode of depression she had experienced six months earlier. She had been very irritable and short with her children, and she recalled Daniel asking, "Why is Mommy sad?" As she thought about it, Karen realized that Daniel's difficult behavior really started then, and got worse only when she returned to work full time, although she herself now felt better. "Perhaps," I wondered out loud, "it's taken Daniel longer than you to recover."

"Should I have let him have the soup?" Karen asked. "It's not about the soup," I replied. In my opinion, there was no "right answer." Either way could have been OK, and each choice had its pluses and minuses, as is true about most of the minute-to-minute decisions we make as parents. What was important, however, was to reflect upon the meaning of Daniel's difficult behavior, to label his feelings and talk about them. My hope was that by giving Karen an opportunity to tell her story, she would learn how to regulate her own distress in future "hot spots" when things began to unravel. If she, in turn, could help Daniel reflect on what was happening, he would learn to say not, "I want soup" but rather, "I feel sad that you're angry with me" or "I miss you when you're away."

A Child's Deepest Need

Being understood by a person we love is one of our most powerful yearnings, for adults and children alike. The need for understanding is part of what makes us human. When our feelings are validated, we know that we're not alone. For a young child, this understanding helps develop his mind and sense of himself. When the people who care for him can reflect back his experience, he learns to recognize and manage his emotions, think more clearly, and adapt to his complex social world. When families come to see me in my pediatric practice for "behavior problems," both parents and children feel estranged and out of control. They are disconnected, angry, and sad. I help them recognize each other. Meaningful change happens when we share these moments of reconnection.

My approach and the ideas behind it have grown out of the unique experience of working on the front lines with children and families in a busy small-town pediatric practice while simultaneously studying contemporary developmental theory and research as a scholar with the Berkshire Psychoanalytic Institute. This research has had direct application to my work and has helped me to help families in dramatic and meaningful ways. I see day after day that if a parent is given the space and time to think about her child's experience, it has a significant and immediate effect on the child's behavior. "Behavior problems" are actually symptoms of disruptions in relationships. My approach can be applied to a wide range of behavioral issues, including, but not limited to, excessive crying, sleep problems, and explosive behavior. As relationships are healed, behavior improves. As children learn to manage strong emotions, parents have an increased feeling of competence. A positive cycle of interaction is set in place. The rapidly moving train of development gets back on track.

Parents are inundated with books on how to solve behavior problems, as well as books on how to raise a child with any number of biological vulnerabilities: the "spirited child," the "shy child," the "explosive child," and the child with "sensory issues." The standard approach in these books is to offer some explanation of the child's behavior, followed by advice about how to handle a variety of challenging situations. These books provide strategies for managing temper tantrums, sibling conflict, or outings to the grocery store. The focus is on "what to do."

In my work with families, I focus not on "what to do" but rather on "how to be" with your child. Guided by the most current research in child development, together with more than twenty years' experience practicing pediatrics, I focus on this one basic point. What a child needs most is to have you recognize and empathize with his experience and help him to contain strong emotions. Whatever quirks and vulnerabilities he may have, they rarely suggest that something is "wrong with him." Rather, they are a unique set of challenges that he must learn to cope with and even perhaps use as an asset as he grows and develops.

Consider Ella, who as a young child was very sensitive to sensory input and overwhelmed by loud noises. She would get agitated and have meltdowns at the most inopportune times. Once when she was three, she exploded at a children's concert where all the other children were quietly sitting on their mothers' laps. At that particular moment, her mother, Beth, might have felt any number of very distressing things, from "what's wrong with my child?" to "I'm a bad parent." She might have yelled at her, or left in a rage, overwhelmed by a sense of shame and failure.

Instead, Beth took Ella to a coat closet next to the auditorium, where she was close enough to hear yet not be overwhelmed. She held Ella on her lap and talked to her about how loud noises were hard for her without conveying a sense that she had been "bad." In doing so she gave Ella the security and the language she needed to think about what was happening to her. In time she might recognize her sensitivities and come to master her distress. Indeed, by age eleven Ella had learned to play several instruments and loved to sing and dance on stage. It is quite possible that her extreme sensitivity to various kinds of noise, which as a young child was such a challenge for her, now manifests itself as a talent for musical endeavors.

Holding a Child in Mind

Research at the intersection of attachment theory, developmental psychology, behavioral genetics and neuroscience is showing that when you can think about your child's experience from the child's perspective, you help your child learn to regulate emotions, solve problems, and adapt to a complex social world. Those who have developed this approach refer to it as "holding a child's mind in mind." For simplicity I call it "holding a child in mind."

What does it mean to hold a child in mind? Imagine this scene, some variation of which has occurred in almost every household with a toddler. Peter sits in his booster seat at the dinner table and insists on drinking from his favorite red sippy cup. But you realize that you left it at the playground that day, so you give him the blue one. He throws it on the floor and starts to scream. How do you turn this moment into one in which he learns to manage his feelings of frustration, rather than one in which he disintegrates into an all-out tantrum and you yell at him and feel like a bad parent?

- The first part of holding a child in mind is to understand his behavior in terms of his level of development. A toddler like Peter is just beginning to develop a sense of himself as separate from you, but at the same time he realizes how small and relatively helpless he is. It is important to toddlers to find any way they can to exert control over their lives, including insisting on a specific cup. Sometimes you may not understand exactly, but simply wonder, "Why is he acting this way?"

- The second component is empathy, which is much more complex than cognitive understanding. It involves both knowing in your mind and feeling in your body what another person is feeling. On a cognitive level, to an adult a cup might be a silly thing to get so upset about. But if you empathize with your child's feelings, you can acknowledge your child's experience, reflecting it back yet showing that while you know what your child is feeling, it is his feeling and different from yours. This helps a child take ownership of his emotional experience and develop a sense of his own mind.

- Holding a child in mind also means containing and regulating difficult emotions. Discipline that accepts the feeling but places limits on behavior can teach a child to manage difficult emotions. In this way a child feels safe, protected from the intensity of his feelings and desires. You might choose to give him a time-out for throwing the cup, which could hurt someone. What you would not do is to run out to the store for another red cup. The idea is to contain the anger and frustration, not make it go away.

- The most challenging component is to think about your child in this way without becoming overwhelmed by your own distress. You might be very angry with your spouse, who is late coming home from work again. You might feel like a failure after leaving a high-powered job and being undone by your two-year-old. Or worse, you might remember that your own father had an explosive temper and would have hit you at a time like this. To hold a child in mind, you must regulate and manage your own feelings, so that they do not get in the way of being present with your child at moments of distress. You may need to work on these feelings before you can take the other steps.

Holding a child in mind can be understood narrowly as an ability to think about your child's behavior in terms of his underlying feelings and motivations. But on a broader level, it is a crucial human skill with long-term effects. Parents who develop this skill are helping a growing child regulate intense emotions. If your child could give words to his experience, he might say, "When you think about me, I learn to understand myself."

Holding your child in mind is sometimes more than a metaphor. Here is a case in point. It was close to 3:00 AM, and Christine's body ached with fatigue. But she was instantly awake when she heard six-week-old Henry stir in his crib. She nursed him in the quiet, dark room, hoping with all her heart that this time he would just settle back down and she could return to her warm bed. But this was not to be. After nursing, Henry began to fuss. Even a good burp did not quiet him. His fussing soon escalated to an all-out cry. Christine held his wriggling body wrapped tightly in a soft flannel blanket. She rocked back and forth, feeling his body begin to relax, only to again be gripped by another round of screaming. She knew from experience that this might take a while. Part of her was screaming, too. "I can't do this anymore! You have to go to sleep!!" But she kept these thoughts under control, knowing that her frustration only prolonged things. And sure enough, eventually the quiet periods lengthened. The wriggling became occasional squirms. She kept rocking, holding him tight in her arms. She sang a song to herself to calm her ragged nerves. Finally that magic moment arrived. She felt him become heavy in her arms as his whole body relaxed. All was quiet. He was asleep. Christine gently returned him to his crib and went back to bed.

The image of Christine physically holding Henry is helpful in trying to grasp the more abstract concept of holding a child in mind. In this physical act one can see the four key elements. First of all, Christine knew that babies of Henry's age may cry for all kinds of reasons; his crying did not necessarily mean that there was something wrong. Thus she understood his behavior in terms of his stage of development. Christine also empathized with the feelings her child was having. She sensed that Henry needed her to be with him, that her presence alone was helpful to him. Third, by literally containing Henry's feelings with her body she was able to help him regulate himself in the face of a difficult experience. She managed to do all of this without being overwhelmed by her own feelings or shutting down emotionally. Christine had had thoughts that she was a bad mother because she couldn't make him stop crying. Her fatigue threatened to overwhelm her and lead her to give up. But she did not shut down. She did not let her distress get in the way of being with Henry.

In my office we see dramatic effects when children feel understood and contained in this way. "She hits him for no reason! We send her to her room, but she just does it again. What can we do to make her stop?" Seven-year-old Amy was in my office with her parents, Lori and Rich, and her three-year-old brother Max. I cringed inside at this all-too-familiar scene of parents asking me to fix their child's "problem behavior." Amy quietly drew pictures at a small table. Her brother played with LEGOS in the corner of the room. "What were you doing?" I asked Amy, referring to the most recent incident of conflict. She began to describe her attempt to enlist her brother's help in tying a rope to a chair to play jump rope. Her mother interrupted. "She just explodes! She pinched him and I sent her to her room." "Let's slow down," I said. I wanted to know what everyone had been doing and feeling leading up to this moment of disruption. As we focused on the details, many things emerged. Lori was overwhelmed by the responsibilities of running the household and acknowledged having little time to think about Amy, particularly since Max was born. Rich spoke of taking many outings with Max and realized that these outings often did not include Amy. "Perhaps she misses me," he said.

As Lori and Rich talked about themselves and how their lives had changed since they had had kids, everyone seemed to calm down. Max began to explore freely all the toys in the room. Amy drew an elaborate picture of a girl on a horse. When I commented on it, Lori began to describe Amy's creativity, telling me that Amy loved to read and to write her own stories.

I felt that some of her rage that had been directed at Amy had dissipated. It occurred to Lori that if Amy had more opportunities to use her creativity, she might not get in so much trouble with her brother. "Maybe she's bored," Lori said. Amy then told us how she wanted to jump rope but that her brother didn't "get" what she was explaining to him.

"Amy is very bright, and also very angry," I observed. "She becomes so overwhelmed by her anger that she can't contain it. It is important that Amy knows that hurting is never OK, but that the angry feelings are OK." We all agreed that being sent to her room for an indefinite period, accompanied by yelling and repeated reprimands, did not help her to calm down. The "time-out" for hitting needed to have a definite structure, with a time limit, preferably a location different from her room, and a clear beginning and end. In addition, Lori and Rich needed to convey a sense that Amy's feelings were understood.

The three of us were engaged in conversation when we noticed that Amy had moved over to the dollhouse and sat beside her brother on the floor. They were playing together. Max handed the dolls to Amy and she placed them on the tiny chairs. They were quiet and cooperative side by side. Mom and Dad stopped talking and watched in awe. "We have never seen this." After allowing some time to let the moment sink in, I said, "They seem to like when you think about them in this way. It makes them feel calm." Our fifty-minute visit was at an end. I acknowledged that we did not have all the answers, and there was still a lot of work to do. But now the family knew what was possible and what to reach for.

As I elaborate upon in later chapters, holding a child in mind may be made more complex by factors that are particular to your child or to you. Among them are your child's biological vulnerabilities, the qualities he was born with, some of which he may have inherited from one or both parents. For example, as we shall see in chapter three, some children, from the moment they are born, have difficulty with what is referred to as "state regulation." They do not easily make the transition from being awake to being asleep and may need to cry intensely to get from one state to another. Others may have extreme sensitivity to sensory input. One infant I took care of would cry when the dishwasher changed cycles.

Further complexity can be added by the relationships in the family, primarily the relationship between two parents. Parents may find it easier to focus on their child's behavior than to face seemingly overwhelming conflict in their marriage. Yet children absorb this conflict and reflect it in their behavior. When you don't feel supported by your spouse, or when parents are not together, handling challenging behavior can be very difficult.

Then there is your own history, particularly relationships with the family you grew up in. When parents associate a child's behavior with difficult episodes in their own childhood, they may become overwhelmed by the fear that their child will suffer as they did. This can make them unable to think clearly just at the moments when their child most needs them. Each of these three components—a child's biology, family relationships, and a parent's history—contribute to any individual "behavior problem."

Research That Led to the Concept of "Holding a Child in Mind"

In England during World War II, as in most Western societies at that time, a mother was thought of mainly as a provider of the physical necessities of food and shelter. The mother–child relationship itself was accorded little value; children were routinely removed from their families to keep them safe, and hospitalized children were separated from their parents for long periods of time. D. W. Winnicott, a pediatrician turned psychoanalyst, was among the first to introduce a different way of thinking. He saw that children developed a strong, healthy sense of self when the people close to them accepted their feelings and helped to manage their emotional experiences. To describe this ideal situation, Winnicott coined the phrase "the holding environment." The way in which a mother makes sense of her infant's expression gives rise to what Winnicott referred to as the child's "true self."

John Bowlby, a British psychoanalyst and contemporary of Winnicott's, observed the devastating effects of separating mother and child. He described the way a child keeps close to his mother in times of stress and fear as "attachment" behavior. Greatly influenced by Darwin, Bowlby postulated that this attachment relationship was essential to the survival of the species. The subsequent forty years of attachment research have clearly demonstrated the wisdom of Winnicott and Bowlby's conclusions. When a parent is fully emotionally available, a child feels free to explore the world with the knowledge that in the face of fear or danger, the caregiver will respond appropriately. On the other hand, if the caregiver is inconsistently available or emotionally removed, as occurs with depression, the child may show insecure attachment. He may be alternately clingy and aggressive in the face of an unreliable or unpredictable caregiver. Furthermore, this research has shown that the quality of a child's attachment to a parent is very closely related to a parent's attachment to her own parents. When an adult describes her relationships to her parents in a way that suggests she is preoccupied or unresolved in some way about those relationships, her child is likely to have an insecure attachment relationship with her.

Emotional availability and holding a child in mind are very closely connected. Peter Fonagy, PhD, a psychoanalyst and chief executive of the Anna Freud Centre in London, and his colleagues found a clear connection between "reflective functioning"—a term Fonagy uses for holding a child in mind— and secure attachment. Parents' ability to think about a child's experience from the child's perspective, to empathize with his feelings, and to contain and help him regulate his emotions without becoming overwhelmed themselves or shutting down is clearly associated with the quality of a child's attachment. Perhaps most important, longitudinal studies spanning more than twenty-five years have demonstrated that when children have secure attachment relationships in early childhood, they are likely to grow up with the ability to handle difficult emotions, think resourcefully, and adapt to complex social situations.

The field known as "behavioral genetics" adds another dimension to these findings. It examines the way in which the environment, specifically early life experience, helps determine how genes are expressed, or turned on and off. The way in which individual genes are expressed in turn determines individual differences in behavior and development. For example, a person born with a genetic trait associated with anxiety may have a large physiological stress response in unfamiliar situations. But if he grows up in an environment that supports him in his efforts to manage these anxious feelings, he may develop the capacity to be comfortable in new situations even in the face of this inherited trait.

Finally, there is a huge explosion of knowledge about the neurobiological basis of emotional regulation, which points to the critical role of the right brain. Even in adults, these structures can be altered in the setting of caring, responsive relationships, such as occur in psychotherapy. Similarly, when parents change the way they relate to their children at times of stress, these critical right brain structures that regulate emotion can change.

Guilt, Blame, and Responsibility

A mother, given time and space, will often move away from a focus on her child's behavior problem, the concern that brought her to my pediatric practice, to talk about herself, telling me vivid stories of emotional distress from her own life. I may suggest that this distress could make it difficult for her to deal with the challenging behavior of her child. Rather than finding this statement helpful, a mother might collapse back into her seat and exclaim in hopeless despair, "Then it's all my fault!" I feel terrible when this happens. My intention was to support her, not to blame her. I have thought long and hard about the reason for this reaction, and I believe the source lies in the three closely related concepts of guilt, blame, and responsibility.

Let's start with guilt. Any parent will tell you that a hefty dose of guilt comes with the job. Where does this guilt come from? It is triggered in large part by the natural but usually unspoken mixed feelings that parents have toward their children. Hundreds of parents, in the privacy and safety of my office, have described being startled by the intensity of rage they feel toward their young child for whom they also feel powerful love. A mother may even confess her disappointment that a difficult child who cries all the time is not the child she dreamed of when she was pregnant.

Children express similar intense feelings. A wise toddler on a popular YouTube video tells his mother from his high chair, "I love you, but I don't like you." And, like the mother who wishes for a different child, he says "I only like you when you give me cookies." Although these experiences can be devastating in the heat of the moment, most parents accept these normal, healthy expressions of frustration and anger. Strong opposing feelings are a part of any passionate relationship.

However, when a parent feels these ambivalent feelings but does not acknowledge and accept them as she does her child's emotions, when a parent believes these feelings are "wrong" or "bad," guilt soon follows. The trip from guilt to blame is a short one. If parents feel guilty simply for having feelings, any suggestion that their actions might affect their child's growth and development will naturally be heard as blaming them when things go wrong. If they feel guilty, they easily assume blame. This kind of guilt can be debilitating. Yet if we acknowledge and accept these mixed feelings in ourselves, rather than being paralyzed by guilt, we can turn this whole idea on its head. Guilt can actually become a thing of value if we realize that "I'm guilty" can also mean "I'm responsible." And "I'm responsible" also means "I can help."

Winnicott summed up these ideas in the following way: "I think on the whole if you could choose your parents . . . we would rather have a mother who felt a sense of guilt—at any rate who felt responsible, and felt that if things went wrong it was probably her fault—we'd rather have that than a mother who immediately turned to an outside thing to explain everything . . . and didn't take responsibility for anything."

Guilt and *blame* are negative words, and *responsibility* is a positive one. People generally feel good about themselves when they take responsibility for their lives. They feel empowered. But taking on the responsibility for raising a child in a meaningful and effective way is not an easy task. In the setting of fragmented families, financial stress, or a parental history of abuse or neglect, it is especially difficult. Add to this a child with a challenging temperament, and the responsibility can easily feel overwhelming.

Though it is not a mother's fault that troubles from her own life may interfere with her ability to respond to her child in the way that he needs, it is her responsibility to address these issues just enough so that she can move them off her child.

The "Good-Enough Mother"

Winnicott, who coined this expression, points out that a mother is most attuned to her child in infancy, when he is most dependent on her, but becomes less so as he grows into a more complex, separate human being. These failures of attunement are not only inevitable, they are in fact a very important part of facilitating a child's healthy emotional development. Winnicott elaborates on this idea in *Playing and Reality*:

> Taken for granted here is the good-enough facilitating environment, which at the start of each individual's growth and development is the *sine qua non*. There are genes which determine patterns and an inherited tendency to grow to achieve maturity, and yet nothing takes place in emotional growth except in relation to the environmental provision, which must be good enough. It will be noticed that the word "perfect" does not enter into this statement—perfection belongs to machines, and the imperfections that are characteristic of human adaptation to need are an essential quality in the environment that facilitates.

Research by psychologist Ed Tronick of Children's Hospital Boston provides evidence that supports Winnicott's idea that the good-enough mother, the mother who fails at times to be attuned to her child, facilitates her child's healthy development. Tronick refers to moments of disruption, similar to Winnicott's "failures of attunement." Tronick and his colleagues video-taped minute-by-minute interactions between infants and their mothers. His research has demonstrated that these moments of disruption can actually enhance development of emotional regulation. Mismatches, when they are recognized and repaired, increase a child's sense of mastery and confidence in his ability to cope with difficult feelings. The accumulated experience gained from dealing with and repairing multiple mismatches, or disruptions, become part of the infant's way of relating to other people. Tronick writes that, "the infant internalizes a pattern of interactive coping that he brings to interactions with other partners. Indeed, to the extent that the infant successfully copes, to that extent will the infant experience positive emotions and establish a positive affective core."

Tronick's research has shown that if a parent is attuned with her infant in only 30 percent of interactions, development will proceed in a healthy way. Even if a mother misreads her infant's cues 70 percent of the time, as long as the majority of these disruptions are recognized and repaired, her child will develop a sense of security and safety in his relationship with her.

I have found that both notions, of the "good-enough mother" and of disruption and repair, have relevance not only in infancy, but for all stages of development. However, while disruptions propel development forward, it is important that they be appropriate to the developmental stage. For a very young infant, having to interrupt nursing while his mother goes to answer the doorbell is a significant disruption. An infant can tolerate this kind of frustration as long as it is brief and his mother returns, and in the tone of her voice acknowledges that she has caused some distress but now she is back and ready to pay full attention to her baby. I have a vivid memory of taking my infant daughter for a walk and mistiming it with her feeding. A few blocks away from home, she began to shriek that high-pitched insistent "I must be fed now" of very young babies. I was sure her cry could be heard all through the neighborhood as I ran stressed and sweating to satisfy her need. We arrived home, and instantly she was quiet and contentedly nursing. Babies in the newborn period can manage these kinds of disruptions and, as I discuss in detail in chapter three, make use of them to learn to regulate reactions to this big new world they are now part of.

An older infant has more capacity to manage his distress and can handle more significant disruptions. In chapter four I address the issue of teaching a baby to sleep independently, a perfect example of the benefit of giving a baby developmentally appropriate frustration. It would not be appropriate to teach a child under the age of four months to sleep independently, because he may not yet have the ability to comfort himself. Starting at about five months, if all has gone well in the preceding months, a baby can begin to regulate himself, grasping a toy, bringing a thumb to his mouth. The sound of a happy baby babbling to himself as he gradually drifts off to sleep is the reward, both for parent and child, of the disruption caused by allowing a few nights of crying. If a child never learns to fall asleep independently, frequent night waking may go on for many years.

In the toddler and preschool years, as a child learns to think about and manage more complex emotions, he is able to make use of more significant disruptions. Consider the story of Carla and George. It was the end of a long day, and Carla was not at her best. A conflict with a colleague at work had left her unsettled, and she was drained and tired. So when her three-year-old son George, whom she knew to have a low frustration tolerance and a tendency to extreme reactions, dissolved on the floor in a fit of hysterical crying when he fell and scraped his knee, she had no patience. "You're being ridiculous," she shouted. "It's just a tiny scrape!" She felt angry and not in control. At the same time, an observing voice in her head told her, "You are not handling this well. You know this is difficult for him and you need to help him." This voice only made her feel worse, blaming herself for her inability in that moment to give her son what she knew he needed. Carla was fortunate that her husband came home just when she recognized this in herself, and she said to him, "You handle this." He sat with George for a while, holding him while he cried, and then he was able to calmly talk with him about his "boo-boo" and reassure him that he was OK.

Later, over dinner, after she had had a chance to regroup, Carla told George that she was sorry she had yelled at him and explained that she was having a bad day. This is a simple example of disruption and repair. As moments like this are repeated, a child sees that a parent can lose her cool, or become "dysregulated," and then recover. He then learns to do the same.

At age three, George needed a lot of help containing and managing his distress. Expecting him to do this on his own would be unrealistic, particularly given his biological vulnerabilities. Yet at age four or five, George's parents might ask him to explain his distress in words, showing him that they were there for him, but that they expected him to be able to manage a minor disruption like this without completely falling apart. In chapters five and six I describe in detail how holding a child in mind in the toddler and preschool years helps him learn to regulate difficult emotions.

In a playgroup of four-year-olds, where children are just learning to contain their aggression and have only the rudimentary skills necessary for social interaction, adult intervention in the face of conflict is essential. On the other hand, a school-age child is better able to manage conflict on his own. It is not uncommon for a child to come home from school with stories of the day's social traumas. It can be difficult for a parent to listen to these stories. A natural tendency for a parent is to want to protect her child, even if it means calling the parent of a child who hurt her child's feelings and demanding an apology. Yet letting a child manage these developmentally normal conflicts, listening and supporting him as he struggles to work things out with his friends, is likely to help him negotiate his way through the increasingly complex social environment of school.

In adolescence, disruptions, both in the social realm and on the home front, can become increasingly dramatic in the face of the intense emotions that go along with this often-tumultuous developmental phase. In chapters seven and eight I show how holding a school-age child and adolescent in mind can help manage these disruptions and move development in a positive direction.

The Aim of This Book

In writing this book, I am supporting you in this task of holding your child in mind. You may come to this book to find out what to do, and I understand this wish to have the answer. But if I tell you what to do, I am the expert. In reality, you are the expert with your child, and you know better than I what to do. What I will help you with, instead, is to develop a new way to think about your child, a new way to be with your child. To quote Arietta Slade, a psychologist at the City University of New York and a leading researcher in this field, "*What to do* will flow easily from that."

The opening words of Dr. Benjamin Spock's groundbreaking book *Baby and Child Care* are "Trust Yourself." In a way this speaks to the importance of positive self-esteem in any significant human endeavor. Trusting yourself as a parent is critical because it gives you a strong place from which to act. Finding that center, that trust in yourself, is not always easy.

I recall working with one mother on the common challenges of having a new baby: sleep problems, difficulty getting her nine-month-old son to accept a bottle, and conflicts with her husband in their efforts to find their way as a threesome. After many months of struggling with uncertainty as a new mother, she had found her center. She spoke to me of a newfound confidence. She had made some decisions about teaching her son to sleep independently. She had elicited her husband's help in weaning. Now that she was able to sleep more than three hours at a time, she could finally think clearly. The low-grade depression that had plagued her since her son was born had lifted. This mother was positively joyful as she spoke of her sense of accomplishment. A month later, however, when I saw her for follow-up, she again seemed crushed, plagued by self-doubt. She rambled from question to question. She was scattered and unsure. "I need to know whom to ask, what books to read," she said. "What you need," I replied, "is to find your way back to that person who was here last time, who believed in herself. Where did she go?"

As we spoke, she identified a number of significant stressors in her life that she realized had thrown her off center. She recognized how much better things went with her baby when she felt sure of herself. She needed to find that self-confidence again.

In this book we will go together, as I do in my office, into the heat of these moments when both you and your child are at your worst, with the aim of helping you find that trust in yourself. I've gleaned these stories from both my life and my pediatric practice. To protect the privacy of my patients, I have created vignettes distilled from hundreds of stories I've been told, with a bit of my own personal experience as a mother thrown in. In some stories, identifying details have been changed. Others are composites of several different families. The majority of these stories are about mothers or mothers and fathers together. This in no way is meant to discount the critical role that fathers play in facilitating their child's healthy development. Rather, it represents the fact that first, in our culture the primary caregiver is usually the mother; second, the vast majority of visits to my office are with mothers; and third, I am a mother.

Reading this book will offer you a space for reflection, analogous to the space I give individual families in my office. My hope is that you will then be free to reflect on your own child's experience. When you have finished reading the book, you will know what it means to hold a child in mind. You will integrate, on the level of your own brain biochemistry, a new way of being with your child, a way that facilitates your child's healthy emotional development.

STRENGTHENING THE SECURE BASE: LISTENING TO PARENTS

S usan and Matt came to see me about their four-year-old son Ryan's explosive behavior. Susan apologized for being late, explaining that she had been up every two hours with their eight-month-old daughter, Emily. Matt looked tense and angry. "There's been some kind of crisis at work," Susan explained. When I inquired about what was wrong, Matt grunted an unintelligible response. So we proceeded and began to talk about Ryan's tantrums. All along I had a nagging feeling that Matt, though he was participating in the conversation, wasn't really there. It made me feel uncomfortable. After about thirty minutes of discussion about Ryan's behavior, when they were both a bit more relaxed, I found an opening. "You know," I said, "since you got here, I've been worried about your crisis at work and wondering what happened." After a quiet moment, Matt looked directly at me and his harsh expression vanished. He described a failing family business and huge amounts of conflict and financial stress. Susan became tearful as she spoke about the effects of this disruption on their daily life. They both wondered how much their stress and sleep deprivation might be affecting Ryan.

Matt may have held back at first, thinking I might be judgmental and blame him for the situation. Instead, when he realized that I was interested in the meaning of his silence, he began to open up. And just as it would have been unproductive for me to press him to respond rather than to try to understand how he was feeling, so Matt and Susan would need to learn the meaning of Ryan's behavior and not just try to change the behavior itself. This is the essence of holding a child in mind.

When parents are told "what to do" without connecting with the feelings behind their experience, both parents and professionals often experience a sense of frustration and failure. Similarly, when parents react only to their child's behavior and not to the feelings behind it, they are frustrated in their efforts to bring about change. In part this is because such "left brain to left brain" interactions occur at the level of thoughts but not feelings. The left brain is responsible for logical, analytic thinking. The right brain, in contrast, is responsible for empathy and it controls the way we regulate emotions. When parents connect with the feeling behind their child's behavior, as I did with Matt, it not only improves behavior, but actually influences the development of the right brain centers that regulate emotions.

Changes in the brain can occur only if the right brain centers that regulate emotion are actually firing. This means that people have to feel something in order to change the way they think and behave. Both in my office and in this book, I try to speak to the right brain. I aim to bring you into the room to join me in these extraordinary moments of recognition between parent and child, when all of our right brains are firing, like the moment when Amy and Max sat side by side playing under the bewildered but loving gazes of their parents.

How the Brain Develops

Contemporary research in neuroscience reveals that a child's brain develops in relation to other people, not simply on its own. When parents are attuned to their child's emotional experiences, new connections are formed that control the way that child regulates her experience. These relationships actually wire the brain. This is particularly true in the first year, when the volume of the brain doubles, but relationships can continue to shape the structure of the brain well into adulthood.

A very brief discussion of the structures of the brain responsible for regulating emotions will, I hope, serve to demonstrate how parents can promote their child's brain development in a healthy way. For the purposes of this book, the subject is greatly simplified. For a more in-depth discussion of this topic, see the works of psychologist Allan Schore, PhD, UCLA School of Medicine, and psychiatrist Daniel Siegel, MD, UCLA School of Medicine, that are listed in the notes. Research at the interface of neuroscience and infant development is offering great insights into how the exchange of looks between mother and baby actually grows the brain. Much of our current knowledge about brain development comes from neuroscience research by such leaders as Nobel Prize winner Eric Kandel. In addition, researchers have learned a great deal about infant development from a combination of detailed video observations of mothers and infants interacting and MRI studies of the brain in action. These imaging studies can actually show which parts of the brain are responsible for what behaviors. This research has shown that healthy wiring of a baby's brain depends on attuned responses of caregivers. These responses can consist not only of words, but also looks, touch, sound of voice, and facial expressions.

A part of the brain called the *medial prefrontal cortex* (MPC) is primarily responsible for emotional regulation. When a person has a well-developed MPC, he experiences a sense of emotional balance. He can feel things strongly without being thrown into a state of chaos. The MPC controls and regulates the *amygdala*, a tiny, almond-shaped structure that is significantly more developed in the right brain and is responsible for processing such strong emotions as terror. Trauma researcher Bessel van der Kolk refers to this area as the "smoke alarm of the brain." This structure, via another part of the brain called the *hypothalamus*, connects with the glands responsible for releasing stress hormones such as adrenaline and cortisol. These hormones give us the physical sensations of stress.

The development of the amygdala begins in the third trimester of pregnancy; it is fully formed at birth. Development of the MPC begins in the second month of life and continues well into a person's twenties. Therapist and teacher Francine Lapides, in a course she teaches called "Keeping the Brain in Mind," describes how by virtue of its location, the MPC literally hugs the amygdala. It serves to regulate and control the smoke alarm and in turn the powerful "fight or flight response."

A third important part of the brain responsible for emotional regulation is the *insula*. The insula, another primarily right brain structure, connects with the visceral organs of the body, including the heart and intestines, as well as the skin. When experiencing empathy for another person, one often has a number of physical sensations, such as a tightening in the chest and tingling in the skin. These physical experiences of empathy, literally feeling what another person is feeling, are mediated by the insula. *Mirror neurons*, a special set of neurons first discovered in the early 1990s, are also thought to be important in the experience of empathy. They activate when a person is either doing something or watching another person doing something. They seem to code for not only the action, but also the goal or intention of the action. Thus they may play an important role in interpretation of the meaning of another person's behavior. The insula, and perhaps the mirror neurons as well, play a critical role in attunement and the sense of being understood by another person.

When these connections are not well developed, intense emotions are not well regulated. In the face of fear, for example, a person may be flooded with stress hormones. However, with a well-developed MPC, she will experience the feeling, but her hormonal response will be turned down so that she is not overwhelmed. If, on the other hand, she does not have a well-developed MPC, the amygdala will go off unrestrained, and she will be flooded with fear that she cannot manage. In the face of overwhelming distress, she cannot make use of the parts of her brain responsible for rational thinking. She may become completely overwhelmed and be unable to function. In fact, the amygdala is overactive in post-traumatic stress disorder (PTSD) and anxiety disorders.

When a parent gazes into her baby's eyes, she literally promotes the growth of her baby's brain, helping to wire it for a secure sense of self. The MPC has been referred to as the "observing brain." It is where our sense of self lies. When a mother looks at a baby in a way that tells her, not with words but with feelings, "I understand you," the baby begins to recognize herself, both physically and psychologically. This mutual gaze, in which the baby is literally and figuratively "seen," actually encourages the development of the MPC and with it her sense of self. As her brain matures in this kind of secure, loving relationship, it becomes wired in a way that will serve her well for the rest of her life. She will be able to think clearly and to regulate feelings in the face of stressful experiences.

Holding Parents in Mind

When I sit with parents of young children, I feel that by connecting with them right brain to right brain, by engaging with their feelings about themselves and their experiences, I help them to shape the healthy development of their child's right brain. When they can become attuned to their child and hold their child in mind, they may create actual connections in their child's growing brain.

To offer this experience to a child, parents themselves need to feel secure. The story of Sam and Donna illustrates the way in which supporting a parent's efforts to hold her child in mind may actually promote emotional regulation. Sam burst into the office, a two-year-old, wild little bundle of energy. Squealing with delight, or was it distress?—it was hard to tell—he ran from toy to toy, not looking at me or his mother and seemingly unable to engage with anything. His mother had brought him to see me in my behavioral pediatrics practice because "he hits me, has explosive tantrums, and I can't take him anywhere."

Donna sank onto the couch in a way that suggested she was feeling discouraged and dejected in her role as mother. She needed to be heard. I sat on the floor, wanting to listen to Donna, but also to include Sam in the visit. At first I focused my attention on her story, while Sam continued his frantic exploration of the room.

Donna described a scene at the playground. The other mothers had been engaged in easy conversation, but she was on edge. She knew Sam was "inflexible" and at any moment could go from happy play to a full-blown tantrum. Sure enough, as she tried to join in the group, she saw him getting upset because his toy car was stuck. She rushed over to calm him, but his crying escalated. As the other kids and moms turned to look, she quickly escalated from embarrassment to rage. She yelled at Sam to cut it out. This only made him scream more. Finally she grabbed him, her bag, and his toys and ran to her car, where she collapsed in tears of helplessness.

Things had not been easy for her. Sam's father had a terrible temper and had been verbally abusive to Donna. He was no longer involved in Sam's life. When she felt Sam's anger, Donna was afraid that he would turn out like his father. Of her own mother she said, "She was never there for me." Donna was frustrated and bewildered by the fact that Sam could relate to other people, but seemed to reserve all his difficult behavior for her.

At the beginning of the visit, Donna had made several awkward attempts to interact with Sam, but without success. She was anxious, and her body language felt intrusive, which seemed to cause Sam to withdraw. However, as she opened up and shared more of these difficult, painful feelings with me, an interesting transformation occurred. Donna's whole body began to relax, and she leaned forward on the couch toward Sam. Sam, in turn, began to engage in more focused play. Donna and I talked about what Sam was doing, observing together how he was calming down. At first he talked to me, bringing me toys and naming them and describing what he was doing. But then he spontaneously ran over and gave his mother a hug. Her pleasure and relief were palpable.

Sam began to engage her in his play and to communicate with her. It seemed as if his mother's newly relaxed attention to him served to calm him down. He could feel her focus on him. She looked directly into his face, speaking with him now in a soft, intimate way. They were engaged in a private dance. As I observed this scene, I felt as if I were seeing Donna growing Sam's brain. Held in a loving way that reflected her recognition of him, Sam was yearning to control his excited emotions. If we as a culture hold parents in mind, that is, instead of telling them "what to do," listen to them and support their efforts to "be" with their child and understand her experience, we not only will help with "behavior problems," but we may actually help to promote healthy brain development.

The Good Grandmother

John Bowlby, describing the essential role of attachment relationships in survival, spoke of a child's need for what he called a "secure base" from which to explore the world and grow into a separate person. He also recognized the need for a mother to have a secure base of her own in order to provide this security for her child:

> I have referred to the ordinary sensitive mother who is attuned to her child's actions and signals, who responds to them more or less appropriately, and who is able to monitor the effects her behavior has on her child and to modify it accordingly. . . . This is where a parent, especially the mother who usually bears the brunt of parenting during the early months or years, needs all the help she can get—not in looking after her baby, which is her job, but in all the household chores. . . . In addition to practical help, a congenial female companion is likely to provide the new mother with emotional support or, in my terminology, to provide for her the kind of secure base we all need in conditions of stress and without which it is difficult to relax.

In some cultures an extended family can fill this role. A supportive grandmother can be very important. If a new mother holds in her mind a warm, loving relationship with her own mother, even if the grandmother is not nearby or is deceased, this relationship can provide the secure base she needs when she becomes a mother.

It is not uncommon in our culture for a mother to raise her children without benefit of her own secure base (and most do not have help with household chores!). Families are fragmented by geography and/or divorce. A spouse may be relied upon both to be the breadwinner and sole emotional support, which can put significant strain on a marriage. Many new mothers I see describe highly troubled relationships with their own mothers, full of grief and loss. I wonder if the immense popularity of "mommy blogs" is the current generation's way of searching for that secure base. But if a mother has experienced significant trauma in her own early relationships, this may not be sufficient.

Sometimes when I sit on the floor with mother–baby pairs and listen to a mother's stories while the child explores the room, I feel that I am somehow in the role of grandmother. I give a mother time and space to relax and be heard, with the hope that this will fortify her in her efforts to be a secure base for her child.

One mother came in with her toddler, collapsed on the couch, and proclaimed, "He's having a terrible day." Her son was very fussy and easily exploded in frustration. But as she and I spoke, he seemed to relax. He climbed off her lap and explored the various toys in the room. At a few moments we could see that he might lose it, such as when his mother told him not to draw on the table with markers, but she was able to redirect him without precipitating a tantrum. When toward the end of our fifty-minute visit I commented on how well he had done, she agreed that he was much calmer than he had been the rest of the day. As was the case for Sam and Donna, there was a kind of cascade effect. As this mother felt held by me, she calmed down and was able to think clearly and focus her attention on her son. As she was better able to regulate her own feelings, she in turn could help him to regulate his. If she can continue to be present with him in this way, she will help his brain develop in a way that helps him to shift attention without dissolving into an all-out tantrum.

This way of thinking about and working with children and families is well described in a relatively new field known as "infant mental health." The field grew out of the work of Selma Fraiberg, a child psychoanalyst who, in her groundbreaking 1974 article "Ghosts in the Nursery," described the Infant Mental Health Program. A staff of experienced psychologists and social workers went into the homes of mothers who had been abused. By forming a close connection in a supportive and understanding way while these mothers were interacting with their children in their own homes, the staff were able to significantly improve the parenting capacities of these traumatized mothers. The most important part of this intervention turned out to be the relationship *between* the therapist and the mother. It was different from therapy with the mother. The aim of the intervention was to help the mother connect with her child in a meaningful way.

In the *Handbook of Infant Mental Health*, Dr. Charles Zeanah, a child psychiatrist at Tulane University School of Medicine and a leading figure in this discipline, cites the definition of infant mental health offered by the organization Zero to Three, which has been widely accepted by the field: "The young child's capacity to experience, regulate and express emotions, form close and secure relationships, and explore the environment and learn." The organization points out that these capacities grow best "within the context of the caregiving environment that includes family, community, and cultural expectations for young children. Developing these capacities is synonymous with healthy social and emotional development." Although in pediatrics the term *infant* usually refers to the first year, this discipline includes prenatal experiences and goes up to age five.

Psychiatrist Daniel Stern and psychologists Tessa Baradon and Alicia Lieberman, among many others, have continued to elaborate upon this tradition. The principles they describe offer a framework for understanding the work I do in my pediatric practice. For example, I have noticed that I often seem to fill a grandmother role. In his book *The Motherhood Constellation*, which outlines the basic principles of parent–infant psychotherapy, Daniel Stern uses the phrase "good grandmother transference" to describe the kind of relationship a parent develops with the therapist who is working with a parent and child together. *Transference* refers to the way people tend to transfer feelings from one relationship, often from childhood, to another, current relationship.

When parents are struggling with their own grief about unresolved trauma from the past, they will likely need to get help, not only to come to terms with their loss, but also to separate their own painful feelings from their interactions with their children. It can be very difficult to keep those frightening feelings in their rightful place. Giving parents space to have their stories heard may free them to be able to see their child's behavior for what it is, rather than its being colored by their own life experiences.

These issues may not emerge right away in a child's life, but rather show up when the child has a symptom that invokes memories of a parent's early life experience. A parent may feel completely at ease with one stage of development, only to become undone as the child moves into a different stage. The help that parents need to hold their child in mind may be discontinuous and intermittent.

For example, Linda, five-year-old Aiden's mom, was having significant trouble managing the sibling rivalry between Aiden and his younger sister. At our third meeting, she began to cry and told me about the death of her older brother when she was a little girl. He had been hit by a truck while crossing the street. She felt that her family had never dealt with the loss and had simply tried to run away from it. Now that she had two children of her own, all the grief came flooding back. She connected her experience with Aiden, particularly his repeated demands to be "first," with her brother's traumatic death. She said, "I'm afraid of Aiden growing up." As Linda began to cry freely in my office, Aiden, who had been quietly drawing on the floor, came and sat on his mother's lap. He handed her a picture he had drawn of a person's face. He said to her (a great example of the saying, "out of the mouths of babes"), "this is you, not me."

During that visit, Linda realized that she needed to address this loss in her own therapy in order to be fully present emotionally with her children in the way they needed her. As she went on to do the difficult but necessary work of grieving over her brother's death, her children were freed from carrying this burden. She could manage their sibling rivalry, which she could now see was typical for children of their age, without becoming overwhelmed by her own distress.

I remember that at the time that I was seeing this family, I was reading Winnicott's paper about development of what he referred to as a child's "true self." It occurred to me that by giving Linda the opportunity to put her grief in its rightful place, I was enabling her to recognize her son's true self. Linda had been substituting her own meaning for Aiden's rivalry with his sister. But once she could recognize the meaning of the behavior from his five-year-old perspective, the problem resolved.

When the Relationship Is the Patient

For many years, I gave community lectures to parents about behavior problems. In these lectures and in my office, I would "explain" their child's behavior. Over my twenty years of pediatric practice, I grew to understand that it was not either the child or the parent, but rather the relationship that was my patient. The relationship is the place where the child's experience, and the qualities she brings into the world, meet the parent's experience. Zeanah writes, "The relational focus of infant mental health has been the sine qua non of this field from the beginning. It is not the infant who is the target of intervention but rather the infant-parent relationship. . . . Instead of the problem or disturbance being understood as within the child or within the parent, the problem may be understood as between the child and caregiver."

The importance of focusing on the relationship rather than the behavior problem that brings families to me becomes clear again and again in my office. Sometimes the nature of the relationship does not appear right away. When eighteen-month-old Kevin; his mother, Amy; and I sat on the floor, Kevin happily explored the toys, returning every once in a while to check in with Amy. Amy explained that she had heard about "time-out" from everyone: parents, parenting magazines, and well-meaning friends. But she could not seem to manage it. When Kevin, not wanting to put on his coat to go outside, took his toy truck and hit her on the head, she felt such an intense flood of rage that she could only scream at him and run from the room. The calm, collected mother everyone seemed to expect her to be in these moments was nowhere to be found. Amy spoke to me of her shock that she could feel such anger toward her child.

About halfway through our visit, Kevin became restless. He had explored all the toys and was eager for some kind of engagement. He picked up a block and made tentative movements to hit his mother with it. "No hitting," Amy said firmly. But Kevin, who had already had experience with her difficulty setting limits to his aggression, did not let up. It was obvious that he was testing her, in a way asking her to set a limit with him. He picked up a small toy, smiled slyly at me, and threw it at his mother.

Amy's whole body tensed as she harshly picked him up and held him tight on her lap. Amy was making every effort to hold herself together in front of me. But Kevin could feel her rage and began to cry, clinging to Amy and burying his face in her chest. After a period of quiet in the safety of my office, where they both had time to calm down, I asked Amy what she was feeling.

She began to cry softly. She talked about her father, who was a quiet man with an explosive temper. She suddenly recalled a vivid memory. Once, when she was about nine, she was having a hard time falling asleep. She tiptoed out into the hall and toward her parents' bedroom. But in the hall she encountered her father, who, she discovered, was not pleased. When she began to complain about having trouble falling asleep, he became enraged. Then to her shock, he slapped her across the face. Tears were streaming down Amy's face as she told me this story, the memory of the pain, both physical and emotional, still fully alive within her. She had never spoken to anyone about this, she told me. The memory lay dormant, only to be released in her new role as mother to this feisty toddler, specifically when Kevin physically hurt her. But until this moment in my office, she had been completely unaware that this was happening.

From Kevin's perspective, he was expressing the normal aggressive impulses of a healthy toddler. But rather than having his feelings contained, he was met by this incomprehensible rage and then emotional absence of his mother, as she retreated to her own painful experience. At home she would literally leave the room, abandoning him. Kevin, in keeping with his persistent temperament, was repeating the behavior. Likely he was hoping for her to stay with him rather than leave him alone. He began to hit more, in a sense searching for an appropriate response to his feelings. Again in the words of Winnicott, he was looking for her to respond to his true self. He needed her to make sense of and contain his aggression. But she was misinterpreting his behavior. He did not mean to hurt her. He was only exploring the boundaries.

If during that visit I were to focus exclusively on Kevin, explaining how toddlers normally hit to express their healthy aggression and how it was her job to set clear limits with him, I would completely miss the problem. Amy was an intelligent woman and was capable of reading the myriad parenting books and magazine articles about limit setting. Such an approach would involve only a left brain to left brain communication. But by connecting with Amy's feelings, or in a sense, with her right brain, I was able to support her efforts to connect with Kevin's feelings. In doing so, she was able to help him regulate his aggression.

Let's think about what might be going on inside Kevin's brain at the moment when he is refusing to put his coat on to go outside. His newly emerging ability to control his environment is threatened. Sensing that he is powerless in the face of his mother's insistence that he put on his coat, his amygdala responds, and he experiences a surge of rage. He feels this physically, as the amygdala sends signals to the hypothalamus and down to the adrenals, causing a release of stress hormones. If his mother does not help him manage this feeling, but instead misinterprets his behavior from the perspective of her own experience and cannot tolerate his anger, he has no way to inhibit his impulsive reaction. She is not available to help him calm down and contain his feelings. So he hits his mother with his toy truck.

Once Amy had discovered the source of her rage, she was able to think about Kevin's behavior from the perspective of a toddler, recognizing his need for limits on his behavior (more about this in chapter five). She was able to be with Kevin in a way that encouraged the development of his brain's regulatory centers. Her calm voice and face, recognizing yet containing his anger, actually result in new connections forming. As Amy continues to stay present in this way over the daily minor frustrations that are part of every toddler's life, she is literally helping Kevin grow the part of his brain, the MPC, that regulates emotions. When Kevin is met with future frustrations, he will be able to regulate his anger so that he can have the feeling, but not impulsively act it out.

To address Kevin's "behavior problem," really to understand what was happening between Kevin and his mother, to support her in her effort to hold him in mind, it was essential to see them together. In that way we could recognize each one's separate experience and see how they came together. By sitting on the floor as a threesome, we created what Winnicott called the "transitional space." This can be difficult to see when there are only two people. Having a third person in the room to watch as the relationship played out made vivid this meeting between individual experiences and histories. Only then were we able to gain a true understanding of what was wrong and support Amy's efforts to be fully present emotionally with her son.

My work with Madison and her mother, Nancy, offers another close-up view of how a parent who feels held in mind becomes able to hold her child in mind. Nancy brought Madison to see me when she was ten months old, with a variety of behavior problems. Madison refused to take a bottle. She fell asleep on the breast and woke every two to three hours to nurse. Nancy laughed nervously as she described the strain these issues were placing on her marriage.

At first, Nancy sat on the couch with Madison on her lap and talked while Madison sized me up, smiling and then turning back to hold her mother. But within a few minutes Madison was squirming. I offered to sit on the floor so Madison could explore. Nancy agreed that this was a good idea, as Madison had recently started crawling and did not like to be confined.

The three of us sat on the floor while Nancy and I continued our conversation. Madison contentedly played with the toy her mother had brought and then began to expand her exploration to the other toys in the office. We proceeded through the history, beginning with Nancy telling me about her pregnancy.

Then I asked about her family. With the same nervous smile she had worn throughout the visit, she laughed and said, "Everything looks perfect on the outside."

I voiced concern about what it was like on the inside. "My mother was severely depressed and frequently suicidal," she said. Tears welled up in her eyes. "I don't want Madison to go through what I did." As she spoke, Nancy was crying freely.

Madison stopped her exploration of the toys. At first she sat completely still, observing her mother. This only made Nancy cry harder, as she saw the effect of her tears on Madison. Then Madison crawled up onto her mother and held on tight. They were both quiet for a bit. Madison began to fuss and reach for Nancy's breast. Nancy got her settled to nurse, and very soon Madison fell fast asleep.

Observing this scene, it became clear to me that Nancy was using the nursing to comfort Madison at those moments when her depression overwhelmed her. Nancy longed to protect Madison from the pain she had experienced in her childhood. Had I simply given her advice about weaning, I would have forced Nancy to abandon the one most reliable means she had to comfort her daughter. It was important to help Madison to separate from her mother and to give Nancy some space for herself and her marriage. We needed to help Madison accept a cup or bottle. But in order to feel comfortable taking this direction, which Nancy fully agreed she needed to take, she would have to find a way to comfort Madison when she herself felt overcome by sadness.

Certainly Nancy needed to get help for her depression. She had been in therapy, and she intended to return. She was on medication. Nancy clearly wanted to begin to wean Madison, both to have time for herself and to ease the strain the baby was placing on her marriage. But the work of therapy can take a long time. What could she do now?

The most painful memory for Nancy was the responsibility she had felt for her mother. Nancy was certain her mother had no idea how she had suffered. But Nancy, by talking with me, could reflect upon Madison's experience. She recognized how her sadness affected Madison. She therefore could acknowledge and reflect Madison's feelings. She, unlike her own mother, could hold Madison in mind. Nancy could communicate, not only with words but with the tone of her voice and the way she looked directly into her daughter's face, that she understood it was frightening for Madison when her mother was sad, but that she would be OK. Madison might not understand the words her mother was saying, but if Nancy could recognize and reflect Madison's experience, that would help Madison manage her distress. Nancy felt less pressure to make her sadness disappear. She saw that she could help Madison even if she herself were still struggling with her own problems. Once Nancy understood how important this was for Madison, some of the debilitating guilt and self-blame she had been experiencing dissipated. This in turn helped her to be more fully present with Madison. Madison, sensing her mother holding her in this way, became less clingy and less irritable. Shortly after this visit, Nancy did in fact wean Madison and was able to help her learn to sleep through the night. These changes in turn had a positive effect on her marriage. A positive cycle of interaction was set in motion that affected the whole family.

In this chapter I have provided multiple examples of how holding parents in mind supports their efforts to hold their child in mind. Parents who feel understood, whether by a family member, friend, pediatrician, or therapist, are in turn enabled to recognize their children's feelings. As we have seen, this in turn helps the healthy development of regulatory centers in their children's brains.

In the following chapters I describe in detail what it looks like to hold a child in mind through each stage of development, from the newborn period through adolescence. I explore the challenges to this task that invariably arise. My hope is that you will recognize yourself in some of the stories in this book, and that your own experience as a parent will be validated, in turn supporting your efforts to hold your child in mind.

LIVING WITH "COLIC": HOLDING YOUR NEWBORN IN MIND

The nurses can tell. "This one's going to be a challenge," they would say to me when I arrived at the newborn nursery to do an exam on the babies born the night before. Anna was one such baby. She would in an instant go from sleeping to an intense, loud, all-out scream. Then the transition back to sleep was just as sudden. I witnessed this myself when, after I examined her, I wrapped her shrieking body tightly in the blanket and walked around the nursery holding her, until suddenly she was sound asleep. The other babies, in contrast, would open their eyes, move around, and make little noises, maybe crying only when I examined their hips, but quieting as soon as I stopped. When I went to see Anna's mother, Helen, she confirmed the nurses' impression: "She cries all the time." Over the next weeks and months, we had many such conversations, as Helen, in the weary haze of caring for a newborn, tried to make sense of this little person.

Deprived of sleep, Helen felt overwhelmed and at times even depressed. Being present with Anna when she had her fussy times and holding her through them was not easy. She needed a lot of support, both from her husband, and in her work with me, to understand that Anna's fussiness did not mean she was a bad mother. Helen recognized that if she could stay calm when Anna was having a hard time, it helped Anna to calm down.

A Mother's Most Important Role

Bringing home a new baby leads to a fundamental reorganization in the way you think about yourself. Trying to understand this new person in your life, in the face of all the other dramatic changes, can seem a daunting task. There was a time when the mother's role was thought to be primarily feeding and physical comfort. But beginning with the work of D. W. Winnicott, more than half a century of research has shown that a parent's ability to reflect and contain her child's experience leads a child to feel safe and secure. This feeling of security in turn leads him to develop a strong sense of self.

When things go well, the newborn period can be a time of bliss. One mother described how her world had narrowed to become simply her and this new love in her life. On her first outing to the grocery store, when her baby was about two weeks old, she was astounded to find that things still went on as usual. Because the primary caregiver is usually the mother, particularly if she is breastfeeding, I refer to the parent in this chapter as the mother. Of course fathers have a very important role to play, and I elaborate on that as well.

What exactly happens between a mother and her new baby during these first few months is so subtle and natural that it can be barely noticeable. Many new mothers, particularly if they have previously had a career, feel that they may lose their minds in the face of the seemingly endless and simplistic tasks of feeding, holding, and diaper changing. But in fact a mother is laying down the foundations of her baby's healthy emotional development.

In a natural way, through her single-minded focus and intense identification with her baby, a mother is exactly tuned in with this tiny being, who in these early weeks and months is completely dependent on her. She knows what he is communicating without words. She interprets his every move and facial expression, recognizing that he needs to be changed, or fed, or simply held. A mother knows. Without effort and unselfconsciously, mothers do this without ever having been taught or learned it through books.

Here is a scene, typical of my visits to the hospital to see newborns, that shows this natural connection. While I was talking with Mark's parents, Seth and Cara, he began to fuss. I was tempted to offer advice: he needs to be swaddled, he needs to be fed. But I kept quiet and simply watched. Cara and her husband exchanged ideas about what the problem was. She stroked the baby's face, tried holding him at a different angle. He continued to fuss. She persisted, talking with him in a calm, soothing voice, remarkably sure of herself given that she had been a mother for fewer than twenty-four hours. We continued our discussion, and after some time had passed we noticed that the baby was sound asleep. "You see," she said to me, clearly pleased with herself. "He was tired."

Winnicott described the first weeks to months of motherhood as a period deserving of a name, a psychological state, which for both a newborn and mother is not only healthy but highly adaptive. The name Winnicott gave this state was "primary maternal preoccupation." He referred to a mother who is preoccupied in this way with her baby as an "ordinary devoted mother." This way of being in tune with the baby happens naturally and does not look like anything particularly dramatic. A mother knows what her baby feels through her intense identification with him. He is a part of her. Though her role is in this sense "ordinary," it is in fact hugely important. Winnicott writes: "It will be observed that though at first we were talking about very simple things, we were also talking about matters that have vital importance, matters that concern the laying down of the foundations for mental health."

In chapter one we saw the extraordinary emotional power of being understood. When someone we love validates our experience, it lets us know that we are not alone. In his work as a pediatrician and psychoanalyst, Winnicott recognized that the original experience of being understood happens in the early months of life, in this powerful connection between a mother and her newborn. He described the way a mother, in her preoccupation with her baby, recognizes what he referred to as the baby's "true self." In a sense we look to re-create this original experience of being understood in relationships throughout our lives. Psychoanalyst Melanie Klein, a major influence on Winnicott's thinking, describes this phenomenon in a poignant manner: "The close contact between the unconscious of the mother and child . . . is the foundation of the most complete experience of being understood. . . . However gratifying it is in later life to express thoughts and feelings to a congenial person, there remains an unsatisfied longing for an understanding without words—ultimately for the earliest relation with the mother."

Sometimes, however, things happen in a mother's life that may interfere with her ability to recognize her child's true self. The story of Jane and Alex shows how a mother may misinterpret a baby's gestures, substituting her own meaning. This can result in a "problem" as mother and baby struggle to connect. Jane called my office almost every day. She was convinced newborn Alex was constipated and that there was something wrong with him. Several doctors examined Alex and told her that he was a healthy, thriving baby. They explained that breast-fed babies often have infrequent stools. But nothing seemed to work. Jane was still worried and felt inadequate, despite extensive reassurance from many professionals.

Then one day she suddenly asked, "Can stress be transmitted in breast milk?" Having heard this from a friend, she was convinced that she had caused what she referred to as "distress" in Alex. The baby's father had left her, and she was feeling overwhelmed. As we spoke I observed Alex, who was lying on his back on the exam table, kicking his legs and making the typical grunting sounds of babies as they begin to experiment with their voices. "See," she said, "he's doing it." "Doing what?" I asked. "He's grunting and pushing his legs because he's constipated." "I think he's talking," I replied. "He doesn't look uncomfortable."

This was a perfect example of how mothers can misinterpret their child's behavior in the context of their own experience. Jane was unable to enjoy Alex's communication because she feared being a failure as a mother. She was in a sense unable to recognize Alex's "true self" because she was substituting her interpretation of his behavior. What Jane needed more than reassurance was a chance to express her fears. My office provided a setting in which she felt safe to say what was really on her mind.

The effect on Jane and Alex's relationship of having this misunderstanding cleared up was dramatic. Once I reframed Alex's behavior for her, she was able to hear the reassurance she had so far resisted. Her fears about his health decreased significantly. She stopped calling my office every day. Jane had a lot to deal with as a newly single mother, and we talked about how she might create a much-needed support system. But her fear and guilt that Alex's behavior indicated she was harming him were gone. When they returned for his two-month checkup, she exchanged smiles with Alex as he lay happily kicking away and cooing on the exam table. She put her face up close to his and said, "I know how much you love Mommy." The delight Alex found in seeing his pleasure reflected in his mother's face was palpable in the room.

The "preoccupation" with a newborn that is essential for healthy development involves not only knowing when to feed or change the baby. A mother's face reflecting back her baby's expression helps him to make sense of what he is feeling. In his biography of Winnicott, Adam Phillips elaborates on this idea:

> When the infant looks at the mother's face, he can see himself, how he feels reflected back in her expression. If she is preoccupied by something else, when he looks at her he will only see how *she* feels. He will not be able to get "something of himself back from the environment." He can only discover what he feels by seeing it reflected back. If the infant is seen in a way that makes him feel that he exists, in a way that confirms him, he is free to go on looking.

Recently I was sitting by a lake with a group of mothers and babies. It was hot and sunny. One mother was trying to tie a hat onto her young infant's head. He was clearly not happy about it. As she held the hat on and secured the strings under his chin, his fussing escalated to an all-out scream. She cooed and talked, reflecting his distress but with a soothing inflection in her voice. In her calm way she communicated with him that she recognized that he was upset, but was confident that he could survive this minor disruption to his day. This is the beginning of the important task for every baby of learning to regulate feelings. This mother was physically caring for her baby while also acknowledging his emotional experience. This helped him to modulate feelings that seemed unmanageable.

Another summertime scene, in contrast, shows what happens when a parent does not contain a newborn's experience in this way. I was on vacation and sitting by a pool, when I noticed a father with his infant daughter. She looked to be about three months old. Perched on a table in her car seat, she sat kicking and smiling. Her father faced her, but was talking on his cell phone. He distractedly shook the rattle hanging in front of her as he spoke in an animated way with the person on the other end of the line. His daughter continued to smile and kick for a while. Gradually, however, she slowed down. She became quiet. Then she began to fuss. Still on the phone, he made more intense efforts to engage her with the rattle. But to no avail; her crying escalated. Finally he had to abandon the cell phone because he needed two hands to take her out of the car seat.

Then he picked her up and held her, walking around the pool in an effort to quiet her, which eventually he did.

It is understandable that a parent would turn to a cell phone or many other ways to cling to that "adult" self that existed before a new little person took over the scene. It may feel terrifying to abandon oneself to a state of total absorption with a tiny being who requires twenty-four-hour-a-day care and does little more than cry, eat, and poop. As we saw in the last chapter, for a mother to be free to provide this mirroring, she herself needs to be held in the way she holds her baby. It's important that she feel free to surrender to the kind of total absorption the baby needs in the first few months.

A mother may find it easier to surrender to this "preoccupation" if she realizes that the need for this intense attunement usually only lasts from birth until the baby is about four months old. By then he is no longer totally dependent. He has begun to learn to regulate himself. He can bring his thumb to his mouth. He discovers that he has two hands that can come together to hold something.

Is It Colic?

Sometimes this newborn period, which mothers have eagerly anticipated in the last months of pregnancy, does not go well at all. A baby seems to cry all the time. Mothers feel helpless. A fussy baby may be difficult to feed. When mothers sense that they are failing in feeding their baby, their feelings of inadequacy go through the roof. One mother told me that in one of her worst moments, after months of listening to her baby scream, she put him down and screamed back, "You hate me!" Parents fight, and marriages are severely strained. Siblings may be resentful, causing parents to feel even more guilty. All of this together may exacerbate feelings of sadness or even depression in a mother. Under these circumstances, the "preoccupation" that a newborn needs may not come naturally. As was the case with Anna and Helen, some mothers need extra support if they are to respond fully to a baby in the way that he needs in order to develop his "true self."

When things are not going well, parents often seek help from their pediatrician. The most common question they have when a baby is crying is, "Does he have colic?" The confusion about this subject results from the fact that "colic" is actually not an illness or disorder, but a description. It means "excessive crying." Somewhat arbitrarily, colic is often defined by the rule of threes: more than three hours of crying a day, three days a week, for three weeks.

Virtually all babies have what is commonly referred to as a "fussy period" toward the end of the day. Having been bombarded with intense sensory input all day, the baby cries as a release to get rid of all the day's tensions. When parents experience the fussing as extreme and disturbing, a search for a "cause" is often undertaken. In a small number of cases, a specific physical problem is found.

There may be an intolerance or even allergy to milk protein. In other instances there is a condition called "gastroesophageal reflux"(GER), in which the acid contents of the stomach go back up into the esophagus, causing pain. The difficulty with this explanation, however, is that all babies spit up to some degree, and many babies who spit up a lot are calm and peaceful. In other words, although reflux occurs in many infants, only a small number will experience it as distressing and cry in response. So even if a problem is found, it is not clear that it is the "cause" of the crying.

Parents often try multiple formula changes, and some attribute the resolution of the crying to a very expensive formula that they finally settle on when the baby is about four months old. However, crying often significantly decreases at this age, so it is difficult to say that the formula is the reason. As a baby's nervous system becomes more developed, he is more able to comfort himself.

I prefer to think of "colic" as an expression of how an infant's nervous system reacts to stimulation from the environment. Rather than think about "what to do" for a colicky baby and how to make it stop, I help parents to "be" with a colicky baby. If we think about colic from the baby's perspective, he is helpless against the onslaught of sights, sounds, touch, and smells around him. His little body and brain do not know how to make sense of what he is experiencing. He needs his parents to help him regulate and contain his feelings. When his mother mirrors his feelings, this does not mean that when the baby is screaming, his mother screams, too. It is more that she shows recognition and acknowledgment of the baby's distress, reflecting back his experience, but in a way that contains it and makes it endurable.

Winnicott describes this way of being with a baby as the "holding environment." The mother's ability to tolerate and contain her baby's distress helps him to make sense of and learn to manage his experiences. Even though holding a baby may seem to be simply a physical act, it is her emotional presence that is important to the baby.

I reframe the crying not as "something wrong with the baby," but rather a normal variation that makes providing this kind of holding more challenging. I try not to give advice about "what to do." As Winnicott so wisely pointed out, the "ordinary devoted mother" knows what to do. Rather, I recognize that these mothers, who are struggling at a time that they had anticipated would be full of joy, are, in Winnicott's biographer Adam Philips's words, "preoccupied with something else." For example, how can a mother be expected to give herself emotionally if she feels that her baby hates her? Loving someone with complete abandon who you feel hates you is simply not natural. In the first weeks and months of a baby's life, many things can lead a mother to be distracted. Given the opportunity to address what is preoccupying her, a mother often feels freed and able to find her way back to that state of "primary maternal preoccupation" so critical to early development.

"Difficult" Babies

Let's take a closer look at the contribution babies can make when these first few months do not go smoothly. Most parents can identify qualities in the baby that make him more prone to cry from the day he is born. Such babies come into the world "wired" in a particular way. Anna showed two characteristics often associated with intense crying. First, she was very sensitive to sensory input, not only to touch, which we observed when I examined her that first day, but also to sounds. On the day I came to discharge Anna from the hospital, she lay sleeping in her bassinet while I spoke with her parents. Suddenly Joel, her father, sneezed. Immediately Anna startled. Her arms flew over her head and her legs extended, and she began to scream. This physical reaction is known as the "moro" reflex. It is a remnant of our evolutionary history, when primate babies had to be ready to reach out to cling to their mothers when startled in the face of danger. It is present in a newborn and gradually decreases over the first several months of life. But for a baby who is sensitive to sensory input, these "startle" reflexes can be frequent and very disruptive. They may cause a sudden, complete disorganization of a baby's nervous system. A baby then needs a lot of help to get reorganized. A mother may have found a few moments of respite, only to find that in the face of such a slight disruption as a sneeze, she must abandon her moment of peace to nurse, swaddle, or rock the baby to quiet him. To make matters worse, some babies with these sensory issues do not like being held. I remember one mother describing how for days she paced back and forth with her screaming newborn, only to discover that when she put him down, he stopped crying.

Babies like Anna also experience difficulty with what is referred to as "state regulation." Pediatrician T. Berry Brazelton and developmental psychologist J. Kevin Nugent, in the *Neonatal Behavioral Assessment Scale*, describe six states of sleeping and waking in a newborn, ranging from deep sleep to awake and crying. Many babies move easily from one to the other in a way that becomes predictable to their parents. But not babies like Anna. They may go suddenly and unpredictably from a "quiet awake" state to an all-out cry. Perhaps they were disrupted by a gas bubble. Because parents cannot see this possible internal disruption, the behavior is bewildering and often incomprehensible. Going from being awake to being asleep is similarly difficult. Whereas some babies may look around, become sleepy, and then gradually enter a deep sleep, others, like Anna, go from an intense crying to being sound asleep and need a lot of help from the people caring for them: being swaddled and held and carried until sleep suddenly arrives.

Anna's mother, Helen, even in those first hours in the nursery, began to feel she was doing something wrong. Her husband and two-year-old daughter sat at the bedside, bewildered by this shrieking creature wrapped in blankets. The point is that although the baby clearly brings this "problem," almost immediately the problem takes on meaning in the context of the family relationships. Mothers feel inadequate, fathers feel helpless, and siblings may feel resentful and alone.

When Helen brought Anna in for visits in the weeks and months that followed her birth, we explored each of these issues.

They came quite frequently in the beginning, because Helen was convinced that there was "something wrong." I would often swaddle Anna in the office and hold her, giving Helen a few moments of respite. Then she could talk and address the reasons it was so very difficult for her to be with Anna in the way she had hoped.

During one visit, we spent most of the time talking about Helen's guilty feelings about the effect of the new baby on Claire, Anna's older sister. Claire was a calm and easygoing child. She and Helen had a very close bond. Yet Anna required so many hours of care that Helen could not possibly be available to Claire in the way she had been. Helen was overwhelmed with sadness at the loss of the intimacy she shared with Claire, who, she observed, had become increasingly needy and clingy.

As we explored this issue in more detail, it became clear to Helen that Claire was reacting not to the baby, but to her mother's sadness. In fact, in the early morning hours, when everyone was calm and relatively well rested, Claire delighted in her new role as big sister. Having the time and space to think about the problem with me gave Helen a chance to recognize the positive aspects of this dramatic change in Claire's life. This in turn lessened her guilt and sadness, giving her an opportunity to enjoy being with Claire in those brief moments of special time when Anna was sleeping and it was just the two of them.

During another visit, when Helen and Joel came together with Anna, we talked about the strain of the baby on their marriage. Joel expressed his resentment that Helen never gave him a chance. If he was holding Anna when she began to fuss, Helen would pace anxiously and then practically grab Anna out of Joel's arms. Helen had not even realized that she was doing this until he brought it up. She in turn spoke of her need for more support from him at the end of the day. They noticed that they had begun to divide the family into two pairs, Anna with Helen and Claire with Joel. They acknowledged that the newfound closeness between Joel and Claire was nice, but they didn't want to be split up in this way. Joel and Helen needed each other to get through this challenging time.

Though we spent time addressing these other issues, we always came back to the fact that Anna was not an easy baby to take care of. As I discussed in the first chapter, thinking about the impact of one's own behavior can lead to guilt or feelings that one is being "blamed." However, we were acknowledging the importance of Helen's ability to be with Anna in the way she needed and the inherent difficulty of the situation given the qualities with which Anna came into the world. This recognition helped to lessen Helen's feelings of inadequacy, which she realized had been interfering with her pleasure in being with her new baby.

Whenever Helen had a chance to bring these problems out in the open and be heard, she felt some release from the burdens she carried, whether it was guilt about Claire, anger at Joel, or debilitating feelings of self-doubt. She realized that she then was more relaxed and fortified in her efforts to be with Anna. Over those first several months, the intensity of Anna's crying gradually decreased. By the time she came for her six-month check-up, there was a sense on everyone's part that the storm had passed. Anna lay on the exam table, kicking and smiling. Helen was thrilled that she had successfully navigated those very difficult months, which in the middle of it all had seemed endless.

A Depressed Mother

The story of Anna and Helen is typical of many I've seen in the course of "well child care." Many such bumps in the road may occur in the newborn period. Sometimes, however, the difficulties of this period are much more serious. When a parent is struggling with depression, providing the intense focus a baby needs in the early months can seem like an unattainable goal. Beth, the mother of three-month-old James, wept in my office. She felt that she was "falling apart." James had been referred to me by a colleague specifically for evaluation and treatment of his "severe colic." Beth had already been to see another pediatrician in my office multiple times and had tried various solutions, none of which was successful.

We met for a full hour visit. While Beth collapsed onto the sofa and shared her story, her husband, John, walked around the office holding the baby, who would cry whenever John sat down. But he seemed more than willing to take on this task, welcoming this opportunity for his wife to get help. I asked few questions, simply offering Beth the opportunity to say what was on her mind.

James was "difficult from day one." He cried all the time, and in fact the crying got worse over the first month. He sounded very similar to Anna. But unlike Helen, Beth had a history of depression. She had been on medication prior to getting pregnant and had resumed the medication after James was born, but still was struggling in the face of this first, very challenging baby. Beth's depression was aggravated by her lack of sleep. That morning, prior to coming to see me, an orange had fallen out of the bag of groceries she was carrying, and she had collapsed on the ground, sobbing.

All Beth could think to ask for was more drugs to ease her emotional pain. She had been to her internist, who had offered to increase her dose of antidepressant. At the same time she knew, in the few moments of clear thinking that she had, that she didn't want to do this. She wanted to understand what was happening and to regain some control over herself and her life. She wanted to find a way to be with James.

John and Beth had been trying for years to have a baby, and in the final months of pregnancy, Beth had had plenty of time to daydream about what her new life would be like. This was not at all what she had imagined. In addition to the chronic fatigue and irritability, she felt incredibly guilty about her wish that James were different, more like the baby of her fantasies.

Beth felt very much alone. John admitted that he, feeling uncertain how to help his wife and son, had retreated to the office and begun to come home later and later. When he did return, tired from the stress of the job, Beth handed him the baby and poured out the trials of her day. She acknowledged that he was her main source of emotional support and understood that this was becoming burdensome to him.

Beth looked to her own mother, who lived on the other side of the country, for help. She spoke on the phone about how she and John were having a hard time. Her mother had never approved of their move away from where she lived and always found a way to make Beth feel guilty about having done so. Beth was hurt and disappointed when at this time of great need, her mother was unavailable, both physically and emotionally. John's mother had died a few years before James was born.

This story is one of "colic" at its worst: a child with a sensitive nervous system, a mother struggling with depression, a stressed marriage, and no supportive grandmother figure to help them through. Clearly Beth needed help with her depression, and I referred her to a therapist. Other than this, I did nothing else but give her the time and space to tell her story. We scheduled a follow-up visit in two weeks.

The next time we met, much to my delight and a bit to my surprise, Beth said that she felt 100 percent better. James continued to have bouts of crying, but Beth felt that she could manage them. She had not gone to the therapist, preferring to spend that time taking a yoga class. She had increased her medication for a few days, but then decided that she didn't need it and was back to the lower dose.

She came into my office grinning at James, who gazed at her from his carrier with adoration. I clearly saw the joy they found in each other. "What do you think made the difference?" I asked. She explained that during our last visit, she felt she was being heard, both by me and by her husband. She sensed that John understood her experience and could support her in a way that felt real and not forced. She also understood that James's intense crying was not her fault and did not represent her failure. With John's understanding, she had the strength to be more responsive to James. In turn, she said, he was calmer.

"I feel as if James were just born," Beth told me. She described a complete transformation in their relationship. Beth had been contemplating going back to work, but was rethinking her plans because she felt that for the first time she and James were really connecting.

I continued to meet with Beth and James about once a month, for there was no doubt that he was a challenging baby, and having a third person to support them was helpful to the whole family. It took the pressure off John to be husband, father, breadwinner, and sole support person. By the time James was eight months old, Beth was a confident and comfortable mother, and she reduced her visits to regular checkups.

The stories I have told in this chapter show what can happen when parents are supported in their efforts to hold their infant in mind. Even when faced with a difficult baby, parents can find their way and be successful. As their babies pass out of this stage of total dependence and begin to learn to calm themselves, their efforts are rewarded. But often parents do not get this support. There may be severe financial stress. Mothers may be raising a child without the baby's father. They may have highly conflicted relationships with their own mothers. In the following chapter we look at the effects of parents' relationships with their own parents on their experience of raising a child.

When I see older children for behavior problems, I often hear stories from mothers who struggled terribly when their children were very young infants. Sometimes the memories are vague, but these mothers often recall vividly the sense of being completely alone. The most dramatic example of this was a mother with severe postpartum depression whose father suddenly died when her baby was three months old. Much to my astonishment, she described being relieved by this event. It wasn't because she didn't love her father. Rather, in sharing the grief with her siblings, mother, and extended family, she no longer felt so terribly alone. In order for mothers to be available for the kind of preoccupation their newborns need, they must not be left alone. If I were to give one piece of advice to mothers, families, and our culture as a whole, it would be to recognize that although what a mother does with her newborn may look ordinary, it is in fact extraordinary and deserves to be valued as such.

If mother and baby successfully manage this state of total dependence, an infant begins to learn to regulate himself. He is no longer completely helpless in the face of his distress. The "good-enough mother" is most attuned to her child in early infancy, when he is most dependent on her. Then the need for this exact attunement lessens. Winnicott writes: "As time proceeds she adapts less and less completely, gradually, according to the growing infant's ability to deal with her failure." Beyond these early months it is not only inevitable, but essential, that a mother gradually fail in her ability to meet her child's every need. As I describe in chapter one, these disruptions, if they are recognized and repaired, propel development forward.

As a child becomes able to regulate himself, he can handle more separation. The first separations, however, are tinged with ambivalence, both for parent and baby. But if a mother has been able to give herself completely to the primary preoccupation of these early months, both she and her baby are ready for the next big developmental challenge, learning to sleep independently.

4

MANAGING SLEEP: HOLDING YOUR INFANT IN MIND

Sara and Tom had not slept through the night for eight months. By day their daughter Maizy was a happy, easy-going baby, but as soon as night came, things would fall apart. Sara would nurse her to sleep around 7:00 PM. Maizy would sleep for about two or three hours, and then, just when Sara and Tom were settling themselves to go to bed, she would wake up crying. She repeated this pattern almost by the clock every one and one-half hours until around 5:00 AM, when she would again sleep for two hours. Of course by this time, Sara and Tom were up for the day. They felt surrounded by friends with babies who "slept through the night" at eight weeks old. They had read books and been given endless "advice" by well-meaning friends and family, but their sleep-deprived haze made it difficult to think clearly. Feeling isolated and alone in their struggles, they came to see me.

Sara had vivid memories of crying out for her mother during the night and feeling terrified at the impending separation bedtime foreshadowed. It was difficult for her to imagine Maizy having the confidence that her parents were there for her if they were in the other room and she was by herself. Determined not to repeat a similar pattern with Maizy, she would go to great lengths to soothe Maizy and avoid hearing her cry. Tom, in contrast, resented the time Sara spent rocking Maizy to sleep repeatedly through the night, time he felt he and Sara should be together. He also saw the effect of severe sleep deprivation on Sara's mood. He felt strongly that they should teach Maizy to fall asleep by herself. But Sara's feelings made it difficult for her to think about the sleep issue from Maizy's perspective.

The First Separation

Managing sleep is one of the greatest challenges of being a parent. It can be filled with intense emotion, as it represents the first major separation for both parent and baby. Parents may feel highly ambivalent about this separation. For a mother who has carried a baby for nine months and then nursed her, perhaps sleeping with her in the bed, the idea of letting her go to sleep all alone in her own crib may be unimaginable. Many mothers have asked me, "How will she manage on her own?" Yet sleep deprivation may cause significant disruption in a family, leading to irritability, strained relationships, and even depression. Holding a child in mind, being present with your child in a way that offers a sense of security, requires regulation of your own emotions, which is particularly difficult in the face of chronic sleep deprivation. Teaching a baby to sleep through the night is a very important task for the overall well-being of a family. However, in the face of ambivalence and doubt, no advice about "what to do" will be of any use.

Offering a Secure Base

If we think of sleep as representing the first major separation for parents and baby, then the work of John Bowlby, father of what became known as "attachment theory," can offer great insight. Bowlby, a contemporary of Winnicott, shared many of his ideas and was influenced by the same social and political climate of England during World War II. Bowlby called the behavior observed between a child and primary caregiver "attachment behavior." He wrote: "For a person to know that an attachment figure is available and responsive gives him a strong and pervasive feeling of security, and so encourages him to value and continue the relationship." Attachment is adaptive and helps keep the child safe. Early attachment relationships actually become part of the child's sense of self and influence her future relationships. As Bowlby puts it, "A young child's experience of an encouraging, supportive and co-operative mother, and a little later father, gives him a sense of worth, a belief in the helpfulness of others, and a favorable model on which to build future relationships."

Hillary sat with her ten-month-old baby, Owen, on her lap. She was on the floor of her friend Dayna's living room with a group of mothers, drinking lemonade and talking. The other babies were exploring the wide selection of toys Dayna had put out, but Owen remained glued to his mother. Hillary chatted with her friends, explaining to them that "he's a bit slow to warm up to new situations, but I know he'll eventually join the group." Sure enough, Owen couldn't resist the allure of a bucket of blocks a few feet from his mother and after a while exercised his newfound crawling abilities and ventured off her lap. All was well until one of the other babies, practicing his cruising skills, reached up to the table next to Hillary and knocked over her glass of lemonade. Instinctively she jumped up and ran into the kitchen to get a towel to dry herself off. It took Owen only a few seconds to register his mother's absence, and Hillary heard his anguished cry from the other room. Another mother came to the rescue and picked him up as Hillary rushed to dry herself off, but Owen's wails only escalated in her friend's arms. Moments later Hillary ran back into the living room. Owen reached for her as his crying almost instantaneously slowed to a quiet whimper. She held him close, offering soothing words of reassurance. "I know you were frightened when you didn't see me, but now I'm back." He again sat quietly on Hillary's lap. "It's OK, she said, "you can stay here until you feel better." Within a few minutes Owen seemed to have recharged, and he resumed his play with the blocks.

This vignette captures the essence of "secure attachment." If Bowlby is the father of attachment theory, Mary Ainsworth, a close colleague of Bowlby's, is in a sense the mother of attachment research. It was her original research that defined the characteristics of secure and insecure attachment.

The Strange Situation

Ainsworth first became interested in understanding what about a parent–child relationship led some children to thrive and others to struggle when she observed hundreds of mother–infant pairs in their home environment. She noticed that there was a relationship between the child's attachment behavior, that is, the behavior she exhibited at times of fear and disruption, and the mother's emotional availability and attentiveness to the infant.

Out of these observational studies Ainsworth designed an experiment to elicit and then measure these attachment behaviors, which she called "the Strange Situation." In this experiment, a one-year-old is observed in a small but comfortable playroom containing a variety of toys in a series of eight episodes, lasting twenty minutes in all. The details of this experiment are very specific, with the goal of making it a research tool with standardized measurements. The child is observed first with the mother, then when the mother leaves her in the presence of an observer who is a stranger to the child, and again when the mother returns. Though the episodes are only three minutes in length, if the child becomes too upset and cannot be comforted by the observer, the episode is curtailed. These encounters were observed through a one-way mirror, and a narrative record was created. A detailed scoring system was devised. The aim was to capture the child's behavior in a way that could be measured and quantified.

Though she expected to see a wide range of behaviors, Ainsworth was surprised to find that the children fell into three distinct categories. The first pattern she called "secure attachment." These infants would use the parent as a base from which to explore. They seemed to expect that the parent would be available, responsive, and helpful. These children got very upset when the mother left, but were quickly comforted by her, and very soon after her return resumed exploration and play. This description captures the relationship between Owen and Hillary.

The rest of the children showed what Ainsworth called "insecure" attachment. One group she called "resistant." Even before the mother left, they seemed reluctant to explore. On her return, they alternated between angry and aggressive behavior and clingy, demanding behavior toward the mother. The other group she called "avoidant." These children seemed to have little interest in the mother. They seemed almost indifferent to her coming and going, often acting more interested in and engaged with the stranger.

What was most interesting about these findings is what happened when Ainsworth observed the same infants in both the home setting and the Strange Situation. The mothers of the infants rated as securely attached in the Strange Situation were consistently sensitive to their child's signals. They encouraged their growing independence, yet they were immediately available when the child appeared to be frightened or unsure. They were loving and responsive when the child sought protection and comfort. The child used the mother as a secure base from which to explore and was able to strike a happy balance between exploration and seeking safety.

The children who showed insecure attachment in the Strange Situation did not use the mother in this way in the home setting. They seemed constantly concerned about where the mother was and were less engaged in exploration and play. They tended to cry more and be more difficult to comfort.

The mothers of the children rated as anxious resistant in the Strange Situation were remarkably inconsistent in their responses. Sometimes they were fully present and available, and at others they seemed distracted and preoccupied. They tended to threaten their child with abandonment when they got angry. The child seemed uncertain whether the mother would be responsive or helpful when called upon. These children were prone to displaying intense separation anxiety and were very clingy and demanding.

The third group of mothers provided minimal to no comfort. Unlike the mothers of the anxious resistant group, who were unpredictable, these mothers of children rated as "avoidant" were consistently unavailable. These children in the Strange Situation seemed almost to behave as if they were completely self-sufficient, but in the home setting they were found to display a large amount of rage and aggression. This pattern seemed to result from the mother consistently turning away when her child approached her for comfort or protection.

In over thirty years of subsequent attachment research, the Strange Situation has become the gold standard for measuring a child's security of attachment. Multiple longitudinal studies that have used the Strange Situation and then followed children from infancy into young adulthood have shown a clear correlation between secure attachment and many elements of mental health, including flexibility, emotional regulation, successful peer relationships, and resourceful thinking.

Exploring Attachment with Adults

Mary Main, a psychologist at the University of California–Berkeley, extended Ainsworth's research, providing evidence for what most parents recognize, namely that the way we interact with our children is very closely linked to our relationships with our own parents. She developed another very important measure for child development research, which she called the Adult Attachment Interview (AAI). The AAI asks an adult to describe in detail his or her early attachment relationships.

Adults rated by the AAI as secure in their attachment to their family of origin might not necessarily have had happy relationships, but they could describe them in a coherent way, and the stories they told described both positive and negative experiences in a way that sounded as if they had come to terms with their experiences. The adults who spoke of insecure relationships with their parents fell into several groups. Some were what Main referred to as "preoccupied." They described difficult, unhappy relationships with their own parents, and they seemed still to be mentally entangled and unresolved in their feelings. These adults easily became agitated when speaking about these relationships, even if the parent was no longer living, and the intensity of the emotion they displayed indicated that these relationships and the conflicts in them were still very much alive. Another group, which Main called "dismissing/detached," might say that they had a happy childhood, but could come up with few specifics and would say they couldn't remember. The few details they did describe did not necessarily sound happy. For example, when describing something like abandonment, there was a lack of connection between the content of what they were saying and their emotional tone.

A third group Main called unresolved/disorganized. These adults had often experienced some significant trauma in their childhood. They often were otherwise high-functioning, coherent individuals, whose speech was dramatically altered when discussing these traumatic events. They seemed to be easily taken away from the present experience of the interview, as if in a way they were for that time living the trauma again. Main described their behavior as "dissociated."

The most remarkable thing about Main's research was the close connection she found between the group parents fell into on the AAI and their relationship with their own children. She administered the Strange Situation to a group of infants and then gave the AAI to their parents. The parents of children who showed secure attachment in the Strange Situation were usually found to describe a secure relationship with their own parents. On the other hand, the children who were found to be insecure in the Strange Situation generally had parents who described insecure attachments to their own parents on the AAI. In fact, parents who were found to be preoccupied were more likely to have children with resistant attachment behavior, and those with dismissing attachment style on the AAI often had children who showed avoidant attachment behavior. Main also added a fourth category to Ainsworth's original three. A small group of children were described as "disorganized" in their attachment patterns, and these were generally the infants of parents rated on the AAI as "dissociated."

Changing Unhealthy Patterns

Contemporary research by Elizabeth Meins, a psychologist at Durham University, England, adds yet another important dimension to attachment research. She and her colleagues have demonstrated that the way a mother thinks about the meaning of her child's behavior during infancy is predictive of her child's security of attachment at one year of age. Meins coined the term *mind-mindedness* to describe a mother's way of attributing thoughts and feelings to her child's behavior. Her group observed six-month-old infants with their mothers in a play situation and measured the number of mind-related comments on the infant's activities that were appropriate to the infant's behavior at the time. This would include comments like, "you want to play with that toy," or giving voice to a fussing baby by saying, "Mommy, I don't want to lie on my tummy anymore." Thinking back to Hillary and Owen, Hillary's comment to her friends about his need for time to get used to a new situation, as well as her statement, "I know you were frightened when you didn't see me, but now I'm back," reflect Hillary's interpretation of the meaning of Owen's behavior. Meins then observed these same mother/infant pairs when the infants were twelve months old in Ainsworth's Strange Situation. She found that the degree of "mind-mindedness" a mother demonstrated was the most predictive of her child's security of attachment. This way of being with an infant offers her the opportunity to begin thinking about her own mind, an ability that, as we shall see in the coming chapters, is critical for emotional regulation and success in the school setting and beyond.

What Meins discovered is full of hope for parents. Looking at Ainsworth and Main's research alone might lead parents to feel resigned to repeating unhealthy patterns of relating from their own families. Meins's research, together with that of others, which I describe in detail in the following chapter, offers an opportunity to understand what exactly is responsible for transmission of attachment from one generation to the next. In other words, if parents can concentrate their efforts on reflecting on the meaning of their child's behavior, they have the opportunity to change unhealthy patterns of relating. As attachment researchers focus on the qualities responsible for secure and insecure attachment, they offer opportunities to change relationships. Repeating unhealthy patterns is not inevitable. By supporting a parent's "mind-mindedness," or ability to hold her child's mind in mind, insecure relationships may be transformed into secure ones in the next generation.

For Maizy and her family, my efforts to help them with their sleep problem focused on recognizing and changing the patterns of relating that Sara had experienced with her own mother. My aim was to support her in her efforts to give her daughter a different experience. Sara's description of her own childhood experiences reflected a sense of insecurity in relation to her attachment to her own mother. The way a parent thinks about letting a child learn to sleep independently is very closely linked to her own early sense of security.

It is important to recognize that the Strange Situation and AAI are research measures, and thus it is never appropriate to label an individual child or parent as having secure or insecure attachment unless she has actually been observed in the standardized Strange Situation or completed the AAI. However,

Main and Ainsworth's research provides a model that helps make sense of relationships.

Sara told me that her mother was only eighteen when Sara, her second child, was born. Sara's father was minimally involved in her life, and her mother was on her own much of the time with these two young children. Sara had vivid memories of how inconsistent her mother was in responding to her expressions of distress. She particularly recalled the sense of fear around bedtime that this uncertainty about her mother had created in her. She had a difficult time imagining that Maizy could feel secure enough in her attachment to Sara that she would be able to comfortably manage the separation involved in learning to sleep independently. When Maizy cried, it brought back those painful feelings of Sara's mother's emotional absence in her times of greatest need. Sara connected this terrible sense of loss with her own desperation not ever to let Maizy cry. But as we spoke, she came to recognize that her distress was more about her own feelings than Maizy's.

Certainly my work with Sara only touched on the surface of her troubled relationship with her mother. But it was enough to help her recognize that Maizy's experience was not her own. Sara was able to move her hurt, conflicted feelings off her daughter. Sara could see that Maizy did in fact have a sense of security in her relationships with both her mother and father. She recognized that in the early months of Maizy's life, she had been attentive to her in the way I described in chapter three. She and Tom had laid the foundation for secure attachment. This sense of security in turn gave Maizy the ability to regulate her feelings and comfort herself. Sara understood that these abilities would help Maizy master the task of falling asleep on her own.

Insight Before Advice

Once we had discussed Sara's own ambivalence and connected it to her childhood experience, Sara began to entertain the idea that she could let Maizy cry at night if it would help her to learn to sleep independently. She was longing for both sleep and a return to the intimacy she had shared with Tom before Maizy was born. But it was essential that she have this confidence in her daughter's secure attachment before we embarked on the "what to do" of teaching Maizy to sleep through the night.

If I had given advice about teaching Maizy to sleep independently without addressing Sara's painful feelings of abandonment by her own mother, I would most likely have failed. But this did not mean I had to help Sara resolve her conflicted relationship with her mother. We just needed to identify these feelings and move them off Maizy. Sara could see that Maizy's life experience already was very different from her own. She saw that she was much better equipped to provide Maizy with the secure base she needed to be comfortable with separation. Sara could then convey to Maizy a confidence that she would be able to manage separation at bedtime.

Much of the difficulty Sara and Tom were experiencing was related to Sara's past relationship with her mother. But that was not the whole story. Both Tom and Sara admitted to their own ambivalent feelings about Maizy growing up. This ambivalence is a natural feeling that all parents have to some degree. While there is the joy of watching your child grow and develop, it is also tinged with sadness about losing the blissful sense of oneness with a newborn. Unspoken ambivalence can maintain a tight grip on a person, and it can be very helpful to have this "on the table" when talking about sleep.

After a couple of visits, when all of these intense feelings were brought to light, Sara and Tom came to an agreement that teaching Maizy to sleep independently would be good for all of them. They understood that from the perspective of her physical development, Maizy was capable of comforting herself. She could hold a toy and bring her thumb to her mouth. They could see the situation from her perspective. She was not benefiting from her mother's extreme fatigue and might feel better if she were able to settle herself to sleep. They could empathize with her experience. They also could imagine tolerating hearing her cry and holding firm to a decision to help her in this way. Similar to the way the mother in chapter three held her fussy newborn to put on a hat, Sara and Tom felt they could tolerate and contain the temporary distress Maizy might experience in learning to master falling asleep on her own. This setting of limits, with the knowledge that the temporary distress a child might experience is a part of working toward a worthwhile goal, whether it be avoiding the sun or getting enough sleep, is a critical aspect of holding a child in mind. And last, Sara could recognize her own anxious feelings about separation and in doing so control her own distress.

From a physiological perspective, it is easy to understand how Sara and Tom got into the pattern of frequent night wakings. For the first eight weeks or so of a baby's life, sleep patterns are disorganized. But starting between two and three months, sleep begins to be organized into a pattern that persists through adult life. Falling asleep consists of a fairly rapid transition from being drowsy (stage I) through stages II and III, into stage IV, which is a very deep sleep. Then for the middle hours of the night, we go through cycles of sleep, from deep sleep to very light sleep, then entering REM (rapid eye movement) sleep approximately every ninety minutes. REM sleep is also referred to as "active sleep" and is the time when dreaming occurs. In the periods both before and after REM sleep, a person is in a very light state of sleep and may be easily awakened. Then in the early morning hours we again enter stage IV, non-REM sleep, for a few hours.

Tom and Sara were blessed with those few hours of quiet at the beginning of the night because Maizy was in stage IV sleep. But when she began to cycle into very light sleep, she searched for the breast in a drowsy, partially awake state, and finding it was not there, became fully awake. Quickly her distress at this situation would escalate to an all-out cry. With this cry she succeeded in getting the breast, and her mother, to come to her.

In a similar way, an adult may sleep with a certain pillow. He may partially awaken and grope around for the pillow, quickly returning to deep sleep. But if someone took the pillow (or it fell off the bed), he would grope around in light sleep. Not finding the pillow, he would become fully awake and might sit up and ask, "Where's my pillow?" The breast and the pillow are what is referred to as a "sleep association," the object (or person) one associates with falling asleep, and which then must be present during these ninety-minute cycles of light sleep in order for a person to fall back into deep sleep. Because Maizy's "sleep association" was her mother's breast, they were stuck in this pattern of frequent night waking.

Armed with this knowledge, what should Tom and Sara do? The "simple" answer is that they need to offer Maizy a "sleep association" that does not require the presence of her mother, so that when she gets to that stage of light sleep during the night, she can fall back to sleep independently. (Weaning off nighttime feeds should be addressed as a separate issue.) The ideal window of opportunity for teaching a new sleep association is between the ages of five and nine months. A baby needs to be old enough to reach for a toy easily and bring her thumb to her mouth. It is important *not* to attempt to teach a child to sleep independently before she has developed the motor coordination to fully control her body in this way. On the other hand, when a child is closer to a year and can stand in the crib and cry "MAMA," the process becomes too difficult for everyone. So five to nine months is an ideal window of opportunity. But it does involve that challenging task of "letting your child cry," and this part is far from simple. To be successful, it is very important that Tom and Sara be in agreement and be willing to support each other through the few tough nights that are inevitable.

Winnicott's concept of the "transitional object," the idea for which he is perhaps best known, can be very helpful for both parents and child in managing this transition to independent sleep. The transitional object refers to a special toy, usually stuffed and soft (and small enough that it poses no suffocation risk), which a young child becomes attached to and then uses for comfort in stressful situations. If Maizy had such an object, it would help Sara and Tom to answer the question, "What will she do without me?" Having observed countless children, including my own, develop such an attachment, I can attest to the fact that there is almost a magical quality to the relationship between a child and her transitional object. For a child, the object is neither part of herself nor part of mother, but something in between that is separate from both, but can represent the safety and comfort of the mother.

When my daughter was five months old, we bought her two soft Puffalumps with a bell inside. She and the toys, which when she began to talk she named "mousey," almost immediately became inseparable. I remember one particular time when she was about two she hurt herself in a fall at the playground and immediately cried out, "MOUSEY!!" Now that my daughter is sixteen years old, the worn and tattered mousies (it is important to have two, both to allow for washing and in case one gets lost) sit on her bed and receive almost no attention, though I suspect she will take them to college. Not all children develop such an attachment, but parents can help things along if they introduce, at around age four to five months, a soft toy (preferably with a twin) and give it to the baby whenever she goes into the crib, either to sleep for the night or for a nap.

After suggesting they introduce some kind of transitional object, I spent some time addressing Tom and Sara's fears that letting her cry would cause Maizy psychological damage. When children learn to walk, they fall down many times, sometimes even hurting themselves. Yet this is an inevitable part of the process. The same is true for learning to sleep independently. It is not something babies are born knowing. They need practice, and that practice can cause some temporary distress. I told them that I could not know for sure what the psychological effects would be, because no matter how much I know about how a baby perceives the world, I cannot be in that child's mind. But we all were in agreement about the ill effects of severe sleep deprivation. Sara was chronically exhausted and irritable, making it much more difficult to be fully emotionally and physically available to Maizy. In addition, the conflict between Sara and Tom about the sleep issue, aggravated by the sleep deprivation itself, was not good for anyone in the family.

I was able to reassure them that babies show absolutely no ill effects from this process. After what may have felt like a highly traumatic night for parents, babies are always their happy selves in the morning. In fact, once everyone has survived the process and a baby has mastered the task of sleeping independently, parents often tell me that their child cries less during the day, is a better napper, and is in general more settled and content. In a sense Tom and Sara were in a position to weigh an unknown—What exactly is going on in my child's mind during those few nights when she experiences some distress?—against a likely positive outcome. For some parents this can be a difficult choice.

The Power of Parents' Choice

I tried my best to convey to Sara and Tom that I was not telling them "to let their baby cry." Rather, I think of it as an informed choice. True, some babies just sleep through the night without having to go through this process. But once a child is Maizy's age and has developed a sleep association that involves a parent's physical presence, she rarely learns to sleep independently without experiencing some frustration and distress. On the other hand, if babies are not given the opportunity to fall asleep independently in infancy, this pattern of frequent waking usually continues for many years. When I see children who are toddlers, preschoolers, or sometimes even older who have always had a person hold or lie next to them to fall asleep, teaching them to sleep through the night can be enormously difficult. Not only do parents have to address the setting of limits and separation anxiety, which are discussed in the following chapters. Learning how to go from being awake to being asleep without the sleep association children have had for many years is a very difficult task. That is why, if parents want to teach a baby to sleep independently, offering a new sleep association during the five- to nine-month window is infinitely easier for both baby and parent.

But for some parents, letting their baby cry is just not an option. There are as many reasons as there are families, but some common themes usually emerge. The first has to do with an infant's biological vulnerabilities. When a child has difficulty with state regulation, her cry may be very intense, and she may persist longer than average in crying before she settles down. Such babies certainly can learn to sleep independently, but parents may get discouraged, particularly if they have friends with babies with more easygoing temperaments who mastered this process in a very short time. The second broad category is parents who perceive their child as particularly "vulnerable." Of course all parents to some degree experience their child as vulnerable, but certain situations can heighten this experience. An increased sense of vulnerability may occur when a couple has had difficulty conceiving and/or lost a pregnancy. A serious illness in early infancy or a suspected problem detected during pregnancy, even if the child is born completely normal, may cause parents to view that child as particularly vulnerable. A third category, and Sara falls into this one, includes parents who are convinced that their child experiences sleeping on her own as being abandoned. Some parents want to understand where these feelings come from and to work through them to the point where they can tolerate hearing their baby cry alone in a crib. This was the case for Sara. Other parents may be so firm in their conviction that they are abandoning their child that they are unable to go through the process.

Once we had addressed Sara's ambivalent feelings about Maizy's separation and their worries about the possible damage the process would cause, Tom and Sara were committed to their choice to have Maizy sleep in her crib. Some parents, however, may choose to have a child sleep with them in their bed, the "family bed." It is important that parents have the option to make this choice without feeling that they are "bad parents." As long as parents are aware of safety issues (no smoking, no soft sleep surfaces, no loose bedding or objects in the bed in which the baby could suffocate), this is a reasonable alternative.

However, this alternative works best if it is made by choice and not forced upon parents because they have not taught their child to sleep independently. If having a child in the bed is simply the path of least resistance and not a conscious choice, usually no one sleeps well. This is particularly true if parents are not in agreement about this issue. The combination of lack of time alone in the bedroom with fighting over where the child sleeps can be quite destructive in a marriage. Often one or both parents will complain that the child moves too much and takes up the whole bed. Usually there is a lack of consistency. After a few nights of letting a child stay in the bed, kicking and wiggling all over, the parents declare that the child must go back to the crib. But when this course of action is met with intense resistance, frequently in the form of loud screaming at 2:00 AM, parents relent, and the child is let back in bed. One of the most difficult situations is one in which some part of the parent, such as an ear, hair, or breast, is needed by the baby to fall back to sleep. A sleep-deprived parent who must offer her body to put her child back to sleep every one to two hours is often an angry, irritable one. For all these reasons, I strongly recommend, as I did with Tom and Sara, that parents give some careful thought to this choice of whether to let a child sleep in their bed. This choice is best made when their child is moving toward that window of opportunity between five and nine months, the stage of development when the child will be most receptive to learning to sleep independently.

A number of good parenting books, including Richard Ferber's *Solve Your Child's Sleep Problems* and Berry Brazelton's *Sleep—the Brazelton Way*, address the "how to" of teaching a new sleep association, as well as related issues such as weaning nighttime feeds and managing interruptions to the process due to illness.

I have gone into some detail about the issue of learning to sleep independently because healthy sleep patterns, both for parents and children, are so important to emotional development. In contrast, sleep deprivation and conflict about the issue of a child's sleep patterns can have a very negative impact on a parent's feelings of empathy toward a child in the coming months and years.

During infancy, when a parent holds a child in mind, she develops a sense of her parent being a secure base from which she can begin safely to separate and explore the world. As we saw, understanding how unresolved feelings in your relationship with your own parents affect your relationship with your child can be very important in helping to provide this secure base.

When everyone is sleeping through the night, it paves the way for success in the often more turbulent toddler years. In this stage, as a child begins to test the boundaries of what she can and cannot do, setting limits is very important. In the following chapter I discuss how holding your child in mind not only helps to change patterns of attachment from one generation to the next, but may also influence the way genes are expressed from one generation to the next.

DISCIPLINE AND LIMIT SETTING: HOLDING YOUR TODDLER IN MIND

Mine is a favorite word of most toddlers. This word doesn't represent greed, but rather the toddler's great joy in his newly emerging sense of self. Children this age delight in their expanding language and motor skills and the new power these skills give them in the world. One particularly exuberant twenty-month-old boy laid claim to everything in my office within his reach and then proclaimed happily, "Run!" as he tottered away down the hall.

The Passionate Toddler

Imagine that your toddler sets his sight on your glasses and declares proudly, "mine." In an appropriate way, you might calmly say, "No, those are Mommy's. I need them to see." Suddenly he is confronted with the fact of his relative smallness and powerlessness. If he happens to be in a particularly vulnerable state, such as before lunch or naptime, he might become enraged that you, his beloved mother, have burst the bubble of his omnipotence. Unable to contain his intense feelings, he might lash out and hit you.

Feeling angry at such an assault is a natural reaction. Yet it's important to contain your own response and to recognize the two-year-old meaning of his behavior. What he needs from you at that moment is twofold. He needs the assurance that you accept his feelings, which you might convey with both a gentle demeanor and a comment about how much he wants your glasses. He also needs to know that you will help him to contain and manage his rage. This might be in the form of a firm statement of "no hitting" or even a brief time-out.

As the toddler in chapter one who declared to his mother, "I love you, but I don't like you," shows us, intense but opposite feelings are a healthy part of any passionate relationship. Bowlby has written extensively on this subject, and his ideas are well summarized by New School psychologist Miriam Steele:

What distinguishes healthy individuals from unhealthy individuals is the extent to which the inevitable conflict between feelings of love and hate, often directed towards the same person, are controlled, regulated and so resolved. For children, Bowlby tells us, this will develop naturally if young children have the loving company of their parents who put up with outbursts of hostility by showing that they are not afraid of hatred and conveying a belief that it can be contained and controlled.

A New View of Genes and Environment

When a child enters the world with genetic vulnerabilities, often expressed at this age as a variety of sensitivities to the environment, empathizing with that child and helping him to manage his experiences can be particularly challenging. For example, a child may be sensitive to taste, which will manifest as picky eating. If a parent herself had similar difficulties, which is often the case, she might find this behavior particularly distressing. On the other hand, a parent who has no such difficulties may find her child's behavior incomprehensible. In these situations the usual battles for control over food choices become exponentially more intense.

Food and eating can be enormously fraught for parents as well as children. Behavior related to food offers a good example of how both genes and relationships are passed from generation to generation. A child may inherit food sensitivities. But behavior about eating is also very closely tied to the way a parent's own family of origin interacted at meals and when eating in general. In this chapter I explore both genetic transmission and transmission of relationships, and how the two are interrelated.

In addition to taste and smell, there is a range of challenges that a child with sensory processing difficulties might face. He might be so bothered by touch that he might need to have the label cut out of his clothes. He might have difficulty with the sense of his body's position; parents describe a child who has no sense of "personal space." A child with poor balance might be clumsy or easily get carsick. Visually sensitive children might fuss about having the lights on or off at night. Sensitivity to sound leads children to become very upset at such things as fireworks and thunderstorms. Working with a child's body—in the form of occupational therapy focused on sensory integration for a young child and for an older child with appropriate activities, including such things as martial arts, swimming, or horseback riding—is an important part of helping him to manage these difficulties.

There is no doubt that being a parent of a child who has any of these sensory processing difficulties is a particularly challenging task. These children are often inflexible and prone to severe temper tantrums. Many, as I described in previous chapters, have these difficulties from early infancy, suggesting a genetic influence. As we are learning, however, a person's genetic makeup at birth does not determine his future. Contemporary research in a field known as "behavioral epigenetics" explores the complex interaction of genes and environment. There is an explosion of knowledge in this area, and for the purposes of this book I offer only a simplified version. (For more in-depth discussion, I refer the reader to the notes, particularly the work of Michael Meaney and Frances Champagne.)

Epigenetics puts a whole new spin on the "nature vs. nurture" debate, which has historically viewed genes and environment as independent factors in determining the course of an individual's development. Rare genetic disorders that result from a single change in the gene sequence have strengthened this misconception. *Epigenetics* refers to changes in DNA structure that alter gene expression, and hence individual characteristics, but that do not involve changes to the sequence of DNA. These structural changes occur when a molecule attaches to the gene and changes the way it is expressed, or turned on and off. According to leading researcher Michael Meaney, PhD, McGill University, *behavioral epigenetics* specifically refers to the way environment, or life experience, influences gene expression and subsequent behavior and development.

Much of the evidence for gene–environment interactions in humans comes from complex, well-designed twin and adoption studies. These studies have shown, for example, that genes associated with antisocial behavior and substance abuse are not expressed in the face of warm, responsive parenting. On the other hand, if parents respond negatively to provocative behavior, the problematic gene is expressed.

The significance of this research for parenting is great. A child may be born with a particular gene for some problematic trait, but the effects of that gene on his behavior will vary according to his environment. Whether or not these genes are expressed, in turn, directly affects the developing structure and biochemistry of the brain. In other words, experience shapes genetic potential, and early life relationships are critical in influencing development of the brain.

To illustrate how this works, I will start with some lessons we have learned from monkeys. Harry Harlow, an American psychologist, conducted research with rhesus monkeys that had a profound influence on John Bowlby's understanding of attachment relationships in humans. Harlow, along with his research assistant, Stephen Suomi, showed that monkeys use their mother as a "secure base" in very much the same way that human babies do. Furthermore, they found that some monkeys have "secure" attachment relationships with their mothers and others "insecure" ones. The insecure monkeys have difficulty regulating fear and are less willing to explore.

Suomi, now chief of the laboratory of comparative ethology at the Institute of Child Health and Human Development in Bethesda, Maryland, acknowledges that "rhesus monkeys are clearly not furry little humans with tails, but members of another (albeit closely related) species." However, they share many important qualities with humans, including forming complex social networks. They share roughly 95 percent of their genes with humans.

Suomi describes two distinct groups of monkeys. About 20 percent of the monkeys he and his colleagues observe both in the wild and in experimental settings are excessively fearful.

They can be identified in the first few months of life. They become highly stressed on a behavioral and physiologic level, with increased heart rate and blood pressure, in the face of any unfamiliar situation. Another group, who make up about 10 percent of the population, have problems regulating aggression. They are overly impulsive and insensitive.

These groups, Suomi explains, also have distinct biological characteristics. The anxious and fearful monkeys have an excess of the hormones associated with fear and increased activity of the part of the nervous system responsible for fear response. The aggressive monkeys have low levels of a certain type of neurotransmitter (a chemical substance involved in communication between nerve cells in the brain) in their cerebral spinal fluid. So far, Suomi's story seems to suggest that the way a monkey is born is its destiny.

But then he tells the second part of the story. Research rearing monkeys under different conditions, some with a consistent, available mother and others without, shows that both genes and early experiences can affect a monkey's levels of fear and aggression. In other words, there may be a genetic vulnerability, but under favorable parenting conditions, monkeys learn to regulate their fear and aggression.

Suomi's research demonstrates that genes exert different influence in different environments. Some monkeys have a gene associated with lower levels of a neurotransmitter called serotonin. Such lower levels of serotonin can lead to elevated fear and aggression. A monkey may have this gene, but in a supportive environment the gene doesn't cause any trouble. The monkey does not show increased aggressive behavior. But in a stressful environment, the gene is expressed, resulting in lower levels of serotonin and increased aggressive behavior.

Suomi's findings on the importance of the nurturing environment in moderating genetic influences have been demonstrated widely in infants, children, and adolescents. Similar to the gene Suomi studied in the rhesus monkey, there is a gene associated with lower serotonin levels in humans. This gene affects stress responsivity and also the structure and function of the amygdala and MPC, which as I describe in chapter two, are critical in emotional regulation. A person may have this gene, but its expression, or its effect on behavior, is strongly affected by life experience. For example, a person with this gene has an increased risk of depression if she experiences stressful life events. Frances Champagne, PhD, a researcher at Columbia University, writes: "Although these examples of interactions between genotypes and early environment are striking, we are only starting to fully appreciate the complex interplay between genetic backgrounds, social environments and brain development. Indeed, it is likely that such interactions [between genes and environment] will be found to be common and significant to the development of most behavioral phenotypes [individual characteristics]."

Let's take a close-up look at "gene–environment interaction" in the story of Jenna. Jenna was a picky eater. She began to have trouble as an infant, as soon as she started eating solid food. She gagged easily, and as she entered her toddler years, she became extraordinarily fussy about eating. Her mother, Maureen, dealt with the issue by insisting Jenna try everything she was offered. But this approach only made things worse. By the time she was three, Jenna became agitated and started to cry when certain things, such as fish, were served for dinner. Her mother Maureen was at her wits' end, sometimes yelling at Jenna, even sometimes forcing her to put the food in her mouth. Jenna would get so distraught that she would spit the food out at her mother. Maureen despaired that she was a failure as a mother.

Maureen's highest priority for her family was that they eat healthy, organic foods. She was a gourmet cook and would spend hours preparing meals for her husband and child. This meant that when Jenna refused to eat them, Maureen would feel hurt and angry. In her own family, she explained to me, there was no choice. Kids simply ate what was served. Maureen couldn't imagine doing it any other way. However, Maureen acknowledged that she was not happy about her relationship with her own parents. She described them as rigid and unloving. It hadn't occurred to her until we spoke that she was imposing on Jenna exactly the highly structured experience that she found so harsh.

Her husband, Tim, had been just like Jenna as a child. In addition to her sensitivities to taste, Jenna was also very sensitive to certain sounds. Both Jenna and Tim were distressed by the sound of a pencil writing on paper. Tim felt bad when Maureen got so upset with Jenna. But he stayed quiet. He recognized the importance of healthy eating to Maureen and was hesitant to confront her because he dreaded having his wife's anger redirected at him. He acknowledged that he had not even recognized that this was happening until we spoke about it. But he became tearful as he thought about both his own painful childhood memories and what this experience might be like for his daughter.

If parents can identify which of their responses bring out difficult behavior, they can make efforts to change these responses, which in turn may modify the way their child's genes are expressed in behavior. Parent–child relationships directly affect gene–environment interactions and can have long-term effects. Tim and Jenna's shared sensitivity to taste and sounds points to a genetic influence. This is not to say that a specific gene for these sensitivities has been identified, but evidence suggests that genes play a role in parent–child similarities of this sort, and their onset early in life suggests an inherited trait. But how is the pattern of relating, or attachment behavior, as exemplified by Maureen's experience with food, passed from one generation to the next?

The Role of Holding a Child in Mind

Research that speaks to the relative influence of genes and environment often includes such phrases as "responsive" parenting, "warm" parenting, or "emotionally available" parenting to describe the kind of parenting that can positively influence gene expression. What does it look like to be "emotionally avail-able?" What does it mean to be "responsive?" The research of Peter Fonagy and his colleagues offers an important answer to this question. It turns out that it is not a mother's behavior, but rather the way she *thinks* about her child, more specifically about her child's mind, that is a key element in transmitting attach-ment patterns from one generation to the next. Fonagy and his colleagues termed this ability to think about another person's mind, or, in other words, to think of behavior as having mean-ing, "reflective functioning." This is an essential element in the kind of child rearing that can overcome the problems brought on by inherited vulnerabilities, as exemplified by Jenna's sen-sitivity to taste.

As I discuss in chapter four, years of research, beginning with Bowlby, had already established that secure attachment in early childhood leads to healthy emotional development. Peter Fonagy and his colleagues wanted to take a closer look. They wanted to know more specifically what elements of par-enting were responsible for the transmission of attachment from one generation to the next.

"I don't want to do to Charlie what my parents did to me." Most parents I see in my office who are struggling with their child's challenging behavior make some variation of that state-ment. Yet they are horrified to find that they are in fact behav-ing in exactly the same way as their parents. They find themselves distracted and emotionally unavailable, or explosive and full of rage, as was the case for Maureen and Jenna. If these researchers could find out what was responsible for this transmission, they could help to change negative patterns of transmission.

Miriam Steele and her colleagues conducted research with adoptees showing that the transmission of attachment security is not genetic. She studied a group of children with a history of serious maltreatment who were subsequently adopted between ages four and eight. Within three months, their play indicated attachment styles that matched their adoptive mothers' level of attachment as measured by the AAI. Although all the children had experienced similar adversity, those whose adoptive mothers described secure attachment relationships with their own parents were better able to manage aggressive feelings and resolve conflict. In continuing studies of previously maltreated adopted children, Steele has demonstrated that though these children still have significant vulnerabilities in attachment relationships, they show remarkable progression in development. If the quality of attachment behavior can change in these very high-risk children, parents can certainly enhance this quality in children without a history of abuse.

In the early 1990s a group of researchers led by Peter Fonagy and Mary Target, a psychologist at the University College, London, initiated a research project that specifically sought to gain a better understanding of how patterns of attachment are passed from one generation to the next. They gave Mary Main's AAI to mothers and fathers while the mother was pregnant with her first child. Fonagy and his group then observed the child in the Strange Situation at one year of age. The first part of the research confirmed what had already been shown. Most of the time there was a match between the results of the AAI and attachment category. Thus if a mother was found during pregnancy to be secure in her AAI, there was a high chance that her infant at one year of age would show secure attachment in the Strange Situation. The results were specific to the parent, meaning that if a father described his relationship with his own parents in a way that was dismissing and detached, his infant would show avoidant attachment behavior in the Strange Situation with him. The very same infant could show secure attachment to his mother in the Strange Situation if she had described a secure relationship with her own parents in her AAI. This was a particularly meaningful finding, because it showed that the attachment category is specific to the *relationship*, not the child. Something happens between a parent and child that results in a secure attachment relationship.

But what is that "something?" When Fonagy and his colleagues pored over the transcripts of the interviews, they found that parents rated as secure not only described the events of their childhood, but they were able to attribute meaning to the behavior of the important people in their lives. They spoke not only about what their own parents did, but how they were thinking and feeling. On the other hand, parents rated as insecure were able only to describe their parents' behavior and did not consistently attribute meaning to that behavior.

A particular subset of questions in the interview specifically asked about this capacity. For example, "Why did your parents behave as they did?" or "How do you think your childhood experience may affect your behavior as a parent?" The researchers rated this ability to think about the feelings and thoughts of another. The scale they created considered "the speaker's awareness of emotional and motivational processes underlying behavior in the self and others." This scale proved to be highly predictive of an infant's security of attachment in the Strange Situation. If a parent was able to think about her own childhood experience in terms of others' feelings, then her child was likely to be securely attached to her. On the other hand, if she did not think about other people's behavior in terms of their feelings, then her child probably showed insecure attachment behavior.

The influence of this ability, even when a parent had an unhappy childhood, was striking. For example, a mother might have had a relationship with her own mother that was emotionally depriving. But if she was able to attribute meaning to her mother's behavior despite her own suffering, she was likely to have a secure attachment relationship with her own child.

Arietta Slade took Fonagy's idea of reflective functioning an important step forward. She described the concept of "*parental* reflective functioning," which refers specifically to the relationship between a parent and child that is currently being formed and still evolving. She developed another research tool, the Parent Development Interview, which looks at a parent's ability to think reflectively about her child, herself as a parent, and her relationship with her child. She describes how a parent's ability to reflect on her child's behavior is both an emotional and intellectual process. It involves not only the ability to empathize with a child's feelings, but to contain and regulate those feelings. In order to be present with her child in this way, a parent must be able to regulate her own feelings in the face of her child's distress.

These elements may sound familiar, as they form the basis of what I have been describing as the four essential features of holding a child in mind, outlined in chapter one: the ability to wonder about and understand, empathize, regulate and contain, and not become overwhelmed by your own distress.

Changing Generational Patterns

Slade offers evidence that a parent's ability to think about the mind of her child, to attribute meaning to the child's behavior, is strongly connected with secure attachment. This ability, which Slade terms "parental reflective functioning," and that I refer to as "holding a child in mind," plays a crucial role in the passing of attachment patterns from one generation to the next.

Just as having a problematic gene doesn't necessarily mean there will be behavior problems, an insecure relationship with one's own parents doesn't necessarily mean that this pattern of relating will be repeated with the next generation. If a parent with an insecure attachment to her own parents is supported in her efforts to wonder about the meaning of her child's be-havior, she has the opportunity to change the pattern of rela-tionships in her family and develop a secure relationship with her own child. Steele's adoption studies offer the most dramatic example of this ability for transformation in attachment relationships.

Let's return to Jenna to see how this research is useful in helping a family. It is likely that Jenna has a genetic vulnerability, represented by her extreme sensitivity to sound and taste. But if her parents can reflect on her experience and understand the meaning of her reactions, not only will they help her to manage these difficulties, but they may even change the effects of the genes linked to her difficulties.

By the time they came to see me, there was all-out war at dinnertime. To help parents in such situations, I always find it useful to go back to the four aspects of holding a child in mind. To understand Jenna's behavior, both of her parents first needed to recognize that Jenna's reactions to food likely had a physical, biological basis. When they saw her behavior in the context of her other sensitivities to sensory input, it made sense to them that she simply could not tolerate certain tastes and textures. In addition, they understood the normal way in which children of her age begin to assert their independence around food choices. It is one area in which toddlers, who see themselves as small and relatively helpless compared to adults, can exert absolute control, because all they have to do is close their mouths.

Second, her parents needed to empathize with Jenna's experience. For Tim, this empathy came naturally, because he had had a similar experience as a child. But Maureen found Jenna's behavior incomprehensible. She needed Tim's help to understand Jenna's feelings.

Third, Tim and Maureen needed to help Jenna regulate and contain these feelings. Setting limits is an essential part of holding a child in mind. As a child starts to assert his independence, he begins to test the limits of what he can and cannot do. Limit setting is not only about controlling your child's behavior; it is about teaching the essential life skills of frustration tolerance, impulse control, and emotional regulation. Setting limits in this situation might begin by acknowledging Jenna's distress over certain tastes and textures, yet not giving her free rein to choose whatever she wanted to eat. Her parents might offer more than one choice at a time, being tolerant of a limited range of options, but not resort to an endless list of possibilities, which are rejected, leading to a situation in which Jenna clearly has the upper hand. Certainly part of the conflict was Jenna's simply wanting to have things her way, as is normal for a child of her age. Balancing respect for her experience with appropriate limits is not an easy task. But children are looking for balance. They like to feel that they have some control, but not too much. Though Jenna likely will not say "thank you for setting limits," if she senses that she is in charge, she may feel anxious. This anxiety will only lead to worsening of demanding behavior. Limits provide a sense of safety and security.

Next, and perhaps most difficult, Maureen and Tim needed to hold Jenna in mind without becoming overwhelmed by their own distress. This meant Maureen's recognizing her history with her parents and her own complex relationship with food. In addition, both parents needed to acknowledge the conflict in the marriage over Jenna's sensory difficulties, which was exacerbated by Tim's history of similar problems in his own childhood. Put this way, the task can easily seem overwhelming. But it is important to remember that all of these issues do not have to be resolved for Maureen and Tim to begin to hold Jenna in mind regarding her issues with food. The issues that were in a sense "in the way" had to be indentified and put in their rightful place. They could then be addressed gradually while Maureen and Tim found ways of handling Jenna's difficulty with tastes and textures.

Kenny is another child whose extreme sensitivity to taste and texture made him as unhappy as Jenna. Kenny had biological vulnerabilities similar to Jenna's. One could say that they had similar "genetic risk." But their environments did not have the same risk. Kenny's mother, Cindy, had a very supportive family who would often say things to her like "just hang in there with him and he'll be OK." There was an uncle who had shown similar sensory difficulties as a child, but was now a professional chef. Both Cindy and her husband, James, had a large support network of friends and colleagues who were very understanding of Kenny's sensory difficulties and tendency to be inflexible and explosive. Kenny's parents were able to appreciate his frustrations and to respond to the reasons behind his behavior. They were tolerant of his restricted pattern of eating and very gradually introduced new tastes and textures. By the time he was ten, he was eating sushi.

Conflicts in the realm of eating behavior that begin in early childhood may play a significant role in our current epidemic of obesity. Sylvia brought her four-year-old son, Andrew, to see me because "he's always eating." An engaging, plump little boy, he was enthralled by the Dunkin Donuts across the street from my office. Sylvia described constant battles around his demands for sweets.

But over the course of our fifty-minute visit, other important issues emerged. Andrew's father, Richard, had lost his job, and the family had moved three times in the past year. Richard struggled with severe depression. In addition to the battles about food, Andrew was having increasing numbers of temper outbursts, and his mother revealed to me that she was at times unable to contain her own rage. She had even on occasion hit him with a belt. As Sylvia became more relaxed and began to open up, she shared that she had been physically abused as a child.

In helping to manage Andrew's out-of-control eating, it was essential to recognize the connection between Andrew's insatiable appetite and the stress he was experiencing in his relationships with both his mother and father. Supporting these relationships was the aim of my work with this family. In addition, both Sylvia and Richard needed help with their own difficulties as they worked to set Andrew on a path toward healthy eating habits. As we have seen repeatedly, it is important to focus on the meaning of behavior rather than simply on the behavior itself.

When parents are supported in their efforts to fathom the meaning of their child's behavior, they have the opportunity to change unhealthy patterns of relating that they may have experienced with their own parents. This is a key to helping parents nurture their child's healthy development. Not only can unhealthy patterns of relating be changed, but it is also possible that by changing these patterns of relating, a genetic vulnerability can become an adaptive asset. Perhaps Kenny, like his uncle, will become a chef.

The story of Kayla and Christine, fraternal (nonidentical) twins, helps to put all of these ideas together. Kayla's mother, Anne, called me when the twins were three because she was having constant battles with Kayla. Kayla's father, Paul, had no such difficulty and actually at first declined to come to the appointment. He reluctantly agreed when I explained that I always prefer to meet with both parents. Kayla had been a difficult child since birth. She never wanted to be held and was sensitive to food, noise, and even the feel of her shirt sleeves on her wrists. She would cry when an airplane passed over the house. Christine, on the other hand, was always a placid, quiet baby and even in the toddler years continued to be remarkably easygoing.

Anne described herself as just like Christine, and she found Kayla's wild mood swings bewildering. She would often lose her temper with Kayla. For example, she had recently taken the girls to a county fair. Christine and Anne had a great time. But not Kayla. She cried in the animal exhibits, complaining that the chickens were too loud. She was afraid to go on any rides.

Anne lost her cool and screamed at her for "ruining their out-ing." Finally Kayla had an all-out meltdown, and they had to go home.

Paul sat quietly during this tale and again asserted rather smugly that he had no such difficulty with Kayla, who was per-fectly well behaved with him. I asked if he had any idea why this was. He told me, "Because I know how she feels." "How do you know?" I asked. "Because I was just like her."

After a moment of silence, Paul began to speak of his own troubled childhood. I wondered if his hesitation about coming to the visit was due to a reluctance to talk about this painful subject. He revealed that he had recently gone to a psychiatrist and started his own therapy. Prior to this experience, he ex-plained, he had felt completely misunderstood his whole life. He would see everyone around him having a good time, and when he couldn't explain what was wrong, he would explode with rage. Not only had his parents reacted with anger, but his father had also on occasion beaten him with a wooden spoon. It turned out that he too as a child had been very sensitive to noise, food, and even the feel of his sleeves on his wrists. Anne then admitted that she feared that Kayla "would turn out like her Dad." Paul and Anne fought about her constantly.

This story reveals how complex the interplay of genes and environment can be. Kayla had bright red hair, just like her fa-ther's. She shared many qualities, both physically and tempera-mentally, with her father. But her behavior varied depending on the environment in which she found herself. Her father could identify with her and thus understand intuitively her experience of the world. He was calm and patient in dealing with her quirks and inflexibilities. Her mother, on the other hand, didn't get it. As we explored the issue further, she revealed a profound sense of inadequacy in relation to Kayla. In fact, she much preferred to spend time with Christine. This was likely not lost on Kayla. It is quite possible that Kayla's behavior was even worse around her mother as she tried in vain to connect with her. Young children do not know how to say, "I feel sad that you are always upset with me." Instead, they often act out in an effort to try to engage emotionally with a parent.

Anne and Paul came to see me because Anne wanted to learn "what to do" about Kayla's "difficult" behavior. Now we all had new ways to think about the problem. The weight of Anne's unspoken fear that Kayla would suffer as her father had done was enormous. They spoke openly for the first time about fears that Kayla's behavior represented some kind of serious mental illness. Now that the fear was out in the open, however, we could tackle it head-on. Paul and Anne recognized the stress this fear had put on their marriage, and in turn on Kayla.

We could agree that Kayla had a "genetic vulnerability" for explosive behavior, likely inherited from her father. But if her parents could provide an environment that was more sensitive and responsive than that in which her father had grown up, her path could be a different one.

Another way to think about it is that Kayla had more than her fair share of aggression compared to Christine. But if she could learn to manage it, it might be transformed into a healthy aggression, often referred to as assertiveness, generally considered to be a positive trait. Certainly Kayla needed to have limits set. Her parents needed to combine a respect for her unique experience of the world with a sense that they could contain and manage her difficult behavior.

Both parents had their work cut out for them. Paul had to manage his guilt about having passed on this trait, in addition to keeping his own emotional difficulties in check. Anne had to work especially hard to feel empathy for Kayla because her nature was so different. Equally important, Anne and Paul needed to recognize the seriousness of this problem in their marriage. They needed to support rather than blame each other, if they were going to help Kayla.

The stories of these families have many complexities, but I hope they make clear how genetics and environment work together in determining the direction of a child's development. When parents realize the importance of reflecting upon their child's experience, there is usually dramatic improvement in behavior. When Jenna's parents reflected on the meaning of her difficult behavior, they were able to help her to calm down regarding the issue of food. Mealtimes are an important period of growth and development for a family. This relatively small change had significant repercussions for the family as a whole. For Kayla and her mother, this reframing of the problem helped them to develop a closer and more loving relationship. This change had other effects as well, on the marriage and the relationship between Kayla and her sister.

It takes a lot of hard work and support for parents to sustain this kind of thoughtfulness and emotional presence of mind. Some parents manage this with trial and error. For the families I describe here, a few meetings with me set things going in a better direction. However, in the face of strained relationships in a marriage or with their own parents, and certainly if they are coping with their own psychological problems, some parents may require ongoing help, such as individual or couples therapy. The rewards of this kind of work are great when a child's development moves in a healthy direction.

A story of three generations may help tie these complex ideas together. Pam was a three-year-old girl who from a very young age had an extreme stress reaction to unfamiliar and potentially frightening experiences. When she moved out of her crib and simultaneously, as kids of this age usually do, developed a vivid imagination, she became fearful of going to bed alone. At the time her mother, Jean, was suffering from severe anxiety and a failed marriage. When Pam came to her room at night, her mother closed the door in her face and told her to "get back to bed." Pam grew up to be an accomplished but highly fearful and anxious person. Her husband, Justin, however, was calm and gentle. They had a daughter, Lucy. When Lucy, who also had a tendency to be fearful in new situations, arrived at their room in the middle of the night after she got her big girl bed,

Pam, with encouragement from Justin, did not shut the door. Rather, she gently took her back to her room, talked quietly with her about her fears, said she knew how she felt, and calmly reassured her that all was safe in her room. She helped Lucy to give words to her experience. As Lucy grew up, although she still had this tendency to be fearful, she recognized it, could name it for what it was, and knew how to manage her feelings.

These three generations likely had a similar genetic vulnerability, with a biologically based tendency to be fearful. There is evidence that such traits are passed on by genetic means. Different life experiences, however, lead to very different outcomes.

The toddler period is a particularly important time for a child to feel understood. By holding her child in mind, a parent first teaches him to think about his own mind. As he goes on to develop increasingly sophisticated language skills, not only can he begin to control his impulses and tolerate frustration, but he starts to be able to give words to increasingly complex emotional experience. Once a child has the ability to think about his feelings, he moves toward managing strong feelings on his own. This skill will serve him well as he negotiates the next developmental step of going to preschool. Being able to think about and understand his own feelings will help him manage both the separation from his parents and an increasingly complex social world.

SEPARATION ANXIETY AND "EXPLOSIVE" BEHAVIOR: HOLDING YOUR PRESCHOOLER IN MIND

The first day of preschool loomed large in Alicia's mind. She found herself dreaming that she would forget to pack a snack, or the alarm wouldn't go off. Her three-year-old daughter, Riley, in contrast, was her usual happy, carefree self. She talked about the first day with excitement, carefully picking out her outfit days ahead of time.

This was Riley's first major experience with separation. Alicia was home full time and had only occasionally left Riley with a sitter. Riley was very attached to her mother, even wanting her close by when she went on play dates. She would often cry out in alarm when she realized her mother was not in the room, though she was easily comforted when Alicia left the group of other mothers and came to where the children were playing. Alicia worried about what would happen when she wasn't in the next room, and perhaps to ease her own worries, wanted Riley to be prepared.

They had gone to visit the school and meet the teachers. Whenever Riley brought it up, Alicia calmly explained that she would leave Riley at school and come to pick her up before lunch. She assured Riley that she would have lots of fun and meet many new friends.

That morning started out well. While they were in the car driving to school, Alicia told Riley what she would be doing at home while Riley was playing with the kids and teachers. She described their plans for the rest of the day. There was a moment of silence, and then Riley said softly, "Why don't we just go home and not go to school?"

Alicia drove resolutely on, though her heart was pounding. In the bustling hallway, Riley stood close by her mother's side. Soon, however, the kind voice of a teacher Riley and Alicia had met during their previous visit broke through Alicia's rising panic. The teacher took Riley by the hand and brought her into the classroom. Another teacher, observing this scene, heard Alicia whisper to herself, "That's it?" "Go," she said gently. Alicia turned and walked away, feeling tears start to well up in her eyes.

Alicia arrived fifteen minutes early to pick up Riley, and the head teacher filled her in on Riley's day. Riley had cried for the first half hour or so. But eventually she had calmed down and soon was showing her teacher the pink nail polish on her toes. When Riley saw her mother, her little lip went down, her arms reached out, and she buried her face in her mother's neck, tears streaming down her face. That evening she proudly told her grandparents, "I went to school!"

Playgroups, too, can present early emotional challenges for children. Three-year-old Evan and his friend Robbie were collecting sticks to roast marshmallows. Evan and Robbie's mothers were best friends, and this marshmallow roast was a highly anticipated part of their regular visit together. But when Evan, who was a very bright but inflexible and easily frustrated child, started poking Robbie with a stick, things began to fall apart. When Evan ignored her request to stop, Dana, Evan's mother, could anticipate what would happen next. She knew Evan would have a hard time when she had to take the stick away. However, she felt calm and confident, despite the wild, screaming protests of her son when she told him he couldn't have any more sticks. She felt the supportive presence of her friend, who she was sure would respect her decision to be firm with Evan despite the disruption it would cause to their afternoon.

Dana took Evan indoors, repeating softly through his cries that she couldn't let him hurt anyone. She reflected his disappointment and acknowledged his excitement about getting together with Robbie. She held him through his escalating screams, feeling a bit embarrassed to have this scene witnessed by her friend, but still able, in the face of these feelings, to focus her full attention on her son's emotional state. She stayed with him for what felt to her like a long time, while his crying gradually slowed to a whimper. Then together they were able to figure out a plan to still have fun that afternoon without using the sticks. They went outside and rejoined their friends.

Learning to Regulate Feelings

The preschool stage is a kind of transition. As a child has the experience of being held in mind, of having her feelings understood, she starts to understand and reflect on her own feelings. Alicia and Dana were helping their children to manage unhappy feelings on their own. During those three hours that her mother left her at preschool, Riley could recognize the feeling of being anxious and fearful. But because she had the ability to think about the feeling, she could regulate herself enough not to be completely overwhelmed. She could keep herself together in the face of distress and be rewarded not only by the fun of preschool, but also pride in her accomplishment.

Evan had some biological vulnerability, bringing intense aggressive feelings and difficulty handling frustration to his relationships. His mother had to work hard to help him manage himself in the face of frustration and not completely fall apart. Yet his experience of being held in mind, of having his feelings understood while having limits set on his behavior, likely will serve to mature Evan's ability to regulate his feelings and eventually handle his vulnerability. Though Dana worried about how Evan would manage at preschool, when the time came she was pleased to discover that he was well able to handle the increasingly complex social interactions he encountered in that setting. Through repeated experiences like the one with Robbie, he learned to manage on his own without his mother. The ability to regulate feelings, a function she had filled for him, became part of him, literally part of his brain structure.

The ability to regulate emotions is essential for healthy development. It includes being able to monitor, evaluate, and modify emotional reactions, both their duration and intensity. When we can regulate emotions, we can still feel things intensely, yet maintain our ability to think clearly and return to a calm state without becoming undone. Without the ability to regulate feelings, in the face of intense emotion a person may even shut down, or become dissociated. As described in chapter two, this reaction occurs in the brain when the medial prefrontal cortex does not regulate the amygdala, and the body is flooded with stress hormones.

We've seen in previous chapters that regulation of feelings develops in the context of relationships. Intense feelings that a child cannot regulate herself can be co-regulated with the help of her parents. Secure attachment and emotional regulation are closely linked. Secure relationships help develop the self-regulatory centers located in the right brain. Being held in mind by a parent leads a child to have that sense of security that in turn gives her the ability to manage strong feelings.

As we saw, this begins in the early months with a newborn literally being held by her mother as she learns to make sense of her physical experience. With the secure sense of attachment that has developed in those early months, an infant begins to separate, developing a regular sleep cycle and learning to sleep through the night. In the toddler years, as her parents set appropriate limits and help her to manage her frustration, she begins to develop an internal sense of her own feelings. By the time a child is three years old, feelings take on a much greater complexity. Not only do children experience frustration and discomfort, but they may also have a clear sense of joy, anger, shame, excitement, and sadness.

Language now plays a critical role in a child's ability to regulate emotions, offering the opportunity to put these feelings into words. But well before children can express feelings in their own words, they can understand their parents' descriptions of their feelings. Not only do parents reflect with their faces and voices their child's experience, they can actually explain what a child is feeling. Narrating a child's experience, for example being able to calmly say, "I understand that you are very angry that we can't get a donut, but we are going home to have lunch," is very important in teaching her to understand and regulate her own feelings. The extent to which families talk about feelings is closely related to a child's ability not only to talk about her own feelings, but also to understand that another person has feelings that are different from her own.

Pretend play during this period also helps support the growing ability for self-regulation. Spend time in any preschool, and you'll find children making up elaborate stories, in which they attribute feelings and motivation to their characters. For example, a child playing with farm animals might tell her teacher, "The cow wants to go into the barn because the other animals don't want to play what he wants to play." Not only does this offer the opportunity to explore other people's minds, but it offers a chance to express feelings that might not be allowed if they were expressed in their true form. One four-year-old girl who had a new baby brother went straight to the dollhouse in my office, took the role of the girl doll, held out the baby doll, and said in a pretend voice, "I'm going to throw you out the window." Pretend play offers children a chance to practice interpreting other people's feelings and to discover that other people have feelings that may be different from their own.

This ability to recognize that other people have feelings that are different from one's own is referred to by developmental psychologists as "theory of mind." It is closely linked to the ability to attribute meaning to behavior. "Theory of mind," according to Peter Fonagy and his colleagues, "is the developmental acquisition that permits children to respond not only to another person's behavior, but to the children's conception of others' beliefs, feelings, attitudes, desires. . . . By doing this, children make people's behavior meaningful and predictable."

Regulating Parental Emotions

To support their children's development in this important area, parents have to be able to manage their own feelings. In the examples above, when Alicia and Dana were working hard to help their children regulate their feelings, we can be sure that they were struggling with their own. They were making good use of the parts of their brain responsible for observing and monitoring their own reactions. Parents may easily become unhinged when their child experiences emotional distress. Alicia had just as much, if not more, anxiety about Riley's first separation as Riley did. But she was able to think about her feelings. Thus the feelings did not overwhelm her, and she was able to offer a calm presence to Riley. This calm presence, this putting aside of one's own distress, is critical if parents are to help children with the big developmental task of separation. Similarly, Dana could manage her own feelings of inadequacy that tantrums often elicit. She could recognize her own feelings of embarrassment, yet manage them enough to be a calm yet firm presence with Evan. This was essential in helping Evan regain control of himself and resume the play date with his friend.

When a child gets to the preschool period and is having difficulty regulating emotions, parents find it very hard to stay regulated themselves. Stress can undermine the ability to reflect on one's own and others' feelings. The parts of the brain that serve to regulate emotions do not work well, and the more primitive parts of the brain may take over. A parent may be able to manage a child's challenging behavior when all is well in her life. But when she is very stressed, her ability to hold her child in mind may collapse. A wide range of things may cause this stress. It may be simply that she is tired at the end of the day. She may have had conflict with a colleague at work. There may be problems in her relationship with her spouse. Or perhaps something about her child's behavior triggers a painful memory of her own past.

Instead of a "dance of regulation" as exemplified by the preceding stories, parents may engage in an unhealthy kind of mutual dysregulation. This can go on for years. For example, if a mother was depressed during her child's early infancy, she may not have been able to reflect her child's experience with her face and voice. If her expressions did not reflect her infant's feelings, but instead were connected with her own distress, the infant's feelings remain confused and thus hard to regulate. Entering toddlerhood without the ability to manage her feelings may lead to difficulty handling frustration. There may be more than the usual number of tantrums, placing further stress on the relationship between parent and child. If on top of this a child has a biologically based difficulty moving from one state to another, which manifests itself as inflexibility as children move from infancy to toddlerhood, or has difficulties processing sensory input, by the time the child enters the preschool stage, things may have spiraled completely out of control.

Sometimes a child will have begun to develop the capacity to regulate her feelings, but if she experiences some kind of significant stress, it may disrupt her emerging skill. The new skill of self-regulation may go "offline." Following are two stories that illustrate these two circumstances.

Regulating Anxiety and Aggression

Mara was at risk of being kicked out of preschool. Her parents, Rick and Ellen, told me at our first visit that she had "personal space issues" and was hitting other children with increasing frequency. They described her as "inflexible" and "explosive," saying she went from zero to sixty in seconds flat. At home they felt that they were walking on eggshells, never knowing what minor frustration might set her off. Her mood swings were rapid and unpredictable. They were both worried that she might have bipolar disorder.

Brenda described how the moment of separation from her son Cole at the start of preschool was "a nightmare every day." Cole would cling tightly to his mother's leg as Brenda spoke in the hall with his teacher. When the moment came for her to leave, he wailed in anguish as the teacher gently pried him from Brenda and led him into the room. Brenda would quickly walk away but collapse in tears when she reached her car, the stress of Cole's anxiety and the guilt of leaving him in such a state flooding over her. During this time Cole increasingly resisted going to bed. Bedtime had become a prolonged event as Cole refused to be separated from his mother. Now he was sleeping in her bed. Cole could not be alone for even a moment and had even begun to follow Brenda into the bathroom.

Cole and Mara's stories are typical of the two most common problems parents come to see me with in the preschool age group: anxiety about separation and explosive behavior. As with Suomi's monkeys, these groups likely represent two distinct genetic vulnerabilities. In fact, there is almost always a significant history of anxiety problems in families of children like Cole and of a range of mood problems, including depression and bipolar disorder, in families of children like Mara. But as we have seen, holding a child in mind may actually change the influence of such genes and so set a child who has a genetic vulnerability on a healthier path of development.

Cole and Mara actually represent two aspects of the same problem, namely the inability to regulate strong feelings. Some anxiety about going to preschool is normal and healthy for a three-year-old. Similarly, some feelings of aggression are healthy and expected, particularly when a child is confronted with the increasingly complex social world of preschool. The problem arises when children do not know how to manage these feelings. They become overwhelmed and flooded with either rage or anxiety. They can no longer think clearly and tend to fall completely apart. When a family brings a child like this to see me, asking "what can we do to manage her behavior?," I help them look for "what is making it difficult for her to regulate her emotions." Whenever possible, I meet first with both parents together without the child. The benefit of this approach is twofold. The parents are free to talk about things they might not want to say in the presence of their child, and they can give their full attention to our conversation without being distracted by the task of looking after their child. After I have acquired a good sense of what the current problem is, that is, exactly what the disruptive behavior looks like, and what parents are thinking and feeling during these moments, I begin at the beginning. I ask parents to tell the story of their child's life, beginning with pregnancy. In addition I explore, to the degree to which parents are comfortable doing so, their relationships with their own parents. As we have seen, these relationships have a profound influence on the way parents think about and relate to their own child. My goal is to support a parent's efforts to be curious about the meaning of behavior and empathize with a child's feelings, in turn helping the child to think about and regulate her own feelings.

When I first saw Mara with her mother, she burst into the office with energy and intense enthusiasm. She eagerly explored every toy in the room. Her mother Ellen seemed on edge, as she anticipated an explosion any time Mara needed to be redirected, such as when I had to ask her not to lean on the window. But in fact Mara handled these moments well. She left the window at my first request and went to play with the dollhouse. Ellen immediately remarked that Mara was much calmer than usual. Perhaps it was because both Ellen and I were thinking about her, and Ellen was more relaxed because I was listening to her.

I asked Ellen to take me into one of the moments of disruption that she so feared. She described an incident the evening before. Bedtime was very difficult, and both Ellen and Rick were already on edge as they anticipated the oncoming struggles. Surprisingly, Mara went willingly into the bath and was having fun playing in the water, when she decided to empty the shampoo bottle. While gently asking her to stop, Ellen reached for the bottle. "No," Mara shouted, grabbing the shampoo and hiding it behind her back. Ellen quickly lost her cool, shouting at Mara, who then dumped out the whole bottle. Rick, sensing that Ellen was not in control of either herself or Mara, tried to take over. But it was too late. Mara began to scream and splash water on her mother. Ellen left the room in tears as Rick lifted wet, struggling Mara out of the tub. She continued to scream and thrash, and Rick feared he would drop her slippery little body. He quickly wrapped a towel around her and carried her to her room. Mara continued to cry and scream for over an hour, resistant to all attempts by her father to calm her. Finally she collapsed in exhaustion and immediately called out for Ellen, who had retreated to her bedroom. Mara insisted Ellen lie down with her and refused to go to sleep unless Ellen held her. The two of them fell asleep together on Mara's bed. This scene was typical, Ellen told me, and similar explosive episodes occurred at least several times a day.

During our first visit, when I met with Rick and Ellen alone, after describing the current problem of explosive behavior, Ellen went on to tell me about her struggle with severe postpartum depression. The first nine months of Mara's life were a blur. When I asked what Mara was like as an infant, she hardly remembered, but Rick was quite clear that Mara was a very difficult baby. When he got home from work, he had to walk with her for hours to calm her. When Mara hit toddlerhood, the challenges continued. It took her forever to pick out a pair of socks because she couldn't stand the feel of the bumps on her toes. Ellen had a relapse of her depression when Mara turned two. She found it very difficult to be with Mara and began to work long hours.

After a pause in the discussion, Rick said thoughtfully, "It sounds like what happened to you when you were two." Initially Ellen laughed this off. But then she told me that her mother had gone back to school when she was two. Her mother was hardly ever home. But the worst part of it, Ellen now recalled, was that her mother was so erratic in her emotional availability, sometimes intrusive and sometimes extremely withdrawn and distant. Ellen was in her own therapy, but had never before connected her difficulties with Mara to her own experience.

At our next visit we talked in a general way about how not having help from your own mother can make motherhood especially challenging. Ellen then sat quietly for a few moments, as if she were mulling over this new way of thinking. Her usually practical, logical tone of voice changed. Ellen said softly, "Maybe Mara needs more of me." She had, until that moment, not let herself think about the intensity of Mara's love for her. It was as if the experience of that love brought back to her, but unaware, the loss of her mother's attention at the same age. She took care of Mara, but her emotions were disconnected and in a sense shut down. Ellen saw that between the depression and her wish not to face the painful feelings associated with her relationship with her own mother, she had been emotionally remote in the face of Mara's distress.

Once all of this had been acknowledged and was out in the open, Ellen found herself much better able to be fully present with Mara in the way she needed. Mara's behavior, Ellen realized, caused her to experience so much stress that she herself felt out of control. Rick had sensed this problem when he came to the rescue in the situation with the bathtub.

It never ceases to amaze me how quickly things can turn around, when at the outset parents feel so lost and desperate. When things go well in my office, it is not only because parents increase their ability to hold their child in mind. Supporting efforts to reflect upon the meaning of a child's behavior is simply the point of entry. Once a child feels understood, or held in mind, she becomes calm. It is likely that this change is on a neurobiological basis, occurring at the level of the structures of the brain that produce stress hormones. When a child is calm, parents begin to feel better about themselves. In fact, often a child's out-of-control behavior *itself* produces a feeling of shame in a parent. When parent and child are more in control, this sense of shame decreases. In turn, when parents feel less shame and less stress, they can think more clearly. They are better able to reflect on the meaning of a child's behavior. Then the child feels even more calm and in control.

Mara's parents' new insight offered a point of entry into the dance of dysregulation in which they had all been engaged. It provided an important opportunity for a new dance. Once Mara felt her parents thinking about the meaning of her behavior, rather than just reacting to the behavior itself, she immediately calmed down. She likely felt understood and recognized. The rapid improvement in her behavior, in turn, decreased Ellen's sense of shame and guilt. She was able to think more clearly in the face of Mara's distress, further enhancing her ability to empathize with Mara's experience.

Both Ellen and Rick began to understand what they needed to do to help Mara to manage her aggression and frustration. We addressed Mara's biological vulnerabilities, exemplified by her sensitivity to sock bumps. Ellen recognized that these difficulties belonged to Mara and were not her fault. She could also feel the distress Mara might have experienced when she herself withdrew, both because of her depression and her longer working hours. Both parents understood that more than ever Mara needed limits set when things began to escalate out of control. And Ellen was able to set aside her own distress at these moments of disruption and address them in her own therapy.

Although an earlier understanding of Mara's feelings would have avoided some of this turmoil, with hard work and consistent attention, the situation can still be turned around. The success Ellen and Rick experienced encouraged them to keep trying to be present with Mara in the way that she needed.

Cole's challenges were quite different from Mara's, but the path to resolution of his severe separation anxiety was similar. Cole had always been a cautious child. Every new situation had to be approached carefully. As an infant, he would be calm in the stroller while it was moving. But if Brenda stopped and they went into a store, he would start to scream. An unfamiliar person would cause a similar reaction. Brenda recalled having been exactly like him as a child. She was extremely close to her mother and was frightened of being alone. She recalled that when left with a babysitter when she was young, she refused to go to sleep until her parents were home. Brenda and her husband, Scott, felt that they had managed Cole's anxiety reasonably well. With a bit of a rough start, he had engaged in preschool and had been doing well.

When we spoke on the phone before our first meeting, Brenda said that she had no idea why things were now suddenly so difficult for Cole. But at the appointment, Brenda recalled that she and Cole had been in a minor car accident. At first Brenda attributed little significance to this event, but she realized that Cole's separation anxiety had become significantly worse in the weeks following the accident.

This visit, to which both Cole and Brenda came, shows one of the benefits of meeting with parent and child together. A child can directly experience a parent wondering about the meaning of behavior. While Cole played on the floor, I asked Brenda to describe what had happened. She was driving with Cole in the back seat when the car in front of them stopped, and she ran into it. No one was hurt, but her car sustained some damage. A friend arrived shortly after and took them home. Brenda sat in the back seat with Cole and quietly wept. Cole had been calm up to this point, but when he saw his mother crying he became alarmed. Brenda recalled that he clung to her and cried out, "Mommy, don't leave!"

We wondered together about what Cole meant by this. It occurred to Brenda that when she became emotionally absent, as at that moment, Cole's separation anxiety significantly worsened. A temperamentally anxious child already, he found himself worried about his mother's well-being.

While Brenda and I were talking, Cole played quietly with the dollhouse in the corner of my office. My attempts to draw him into the conversation were unsuccessful, but clearly he was listening. Toward the end of the visit he acted out a scene with the dolls with the parents putting them to bed and everyone going off to sleep. Brenda was surprised to see this play. She commented that Cole seemed to be acting out what he wished were true.

Both Brenda and I now understood what had happened. Brenda no longer felt that Cole's behavior was incomprehensible. Cole's increase in anxiety made sense. It was as if in that moment in the car he had felt himself dropped from his mother's mind as she became overwhelmed by her own distress. The stress of this experience caused him to lose his newly found ability to contain his anxiety. Things went rapidly downhill from there. Cole's increased anxiety led to the sleep disruption, which affected everyone's ability to think clearly.

Once Brenda was able to understand what the experience of the accident had been from Cole's perspective, she saw where his distress came from, and so his behavior made sense. Because Brenda and Scott had felt helpless in the face of his anxiety, they had become very lax about setting limits at bedtime. Now they reinstituted these limits, but at the same time provided the reassurance that he needed that his parents wouldn't leave him. This combination of reassurance and limits helped Cole to contain his anxiety. As a result everyone was sleeping better. Brenda, relieved of the guilt she had been feeling, was able to reassure Cole calmly when she dropped him off at school. Cole's ability to manage his feelings came back "online" once the trauma had been addressed.

Mara and Cole gradually became able to learn to regulate their feelings. Rather than responding only to the behavior itself, their parents learned to wonder about its meaning. Certainly there were bumps in the road when each child's behavior again escalated out of control. But both their families knew when they needed help and would come in for a consultation when they hit these bumps. Both children went on to do well in school.

Support for Parents

When parents feel supported in holding their child in mind, the way is paved for a successful transition to preschool. But many parent–child pairs I have met unfortunately do not get this opportunity. I first saw Robin when she was three years old. Her mother, Heather, described an extraordinarily difficult first year. Robin was her second child, born when her first was fifteen months old. Heather's husband, Mark, worked several jobs and was rarely home. When he was, his explosive temper often frightened Heather. She recalled being very depressed and alone. Unlike her first child, Robin was a very difficult baby who needed to be held all the time and was difficult to feed. When we first met, Heather described an explosive child whom she felt she could not control. She spoke of a troubled marriage and estrangement from her mother, with whom she had once been close. Given the stresses on both Heather and her marriage, I recommended family counseling.

I did not see Robin and Heather until a year later. The financial stress had forced her to take a full-time job, and she could not find the time to come to see me. She could not find a family therapist who accepted their insurance, and even if she had found one, she felt that she had neither the time nor a willing partner. Mark did not approve of talking to any outside person, even me, about the troubles they were experiencing at home. Robin's behavior had become worse, and she was at risk of being kicked out of preschool. My efforts to help were thwarted by Mark's refusal to participate. Robin and Heather came once and then did not call again.

Yet another year later, when Robin entered kindergarten, her mother brought her to see a child psychiatrist who, upon one visit with only Robin and Heather (Mark was not present) diagnosed attention deficit hyperactivity disorder (ADHD) and recommended medication. At first Heather resisted, but when Robin entered first grade, she was unable to attend to the teacher and her behavior was so impulsive that Heather felt she had no choice. And at that point it is quite possible that medication would have helped Robin to be able to listen in class. I cannot help but wonder whether, if Heather had had the support she needed when Robin was an infant, if the family could have found help when her problems first began, her path would have been different. I address these obstacles to getting necessary care in detail in the last chapter.

The stories in this chapter represent the range of possibilities as a child begins to learn to regulate her own emotions. Many parents have enough ability to manage their own emotions, which enables them, often with the support of family and friends, to understand their child's perspective and be fully present in a way their preschool-age child needs. When things have not gone so well, either from early infancy or because of some kind of trauma, parents can, with help, work to set their child on a healthy path of development. If not, as we see in the story of Robin and Heather, when the stresses are too great and help is unavailable, a child may be unable to cope with the complex challenges of preschool, and problems with behavior and emotional regulation continue.

Parents continue throughout a child's development to solidify the child's ability to think about her feelings and regulate emotions. In addition, the supportive environment of preschool gives her the opportunity to practice this new skill as she manages separation and increasingly complex social interaction. Preschool teachers have an important role to play in continuing a child's education in self-regulation and understanding of others' feelings. Both of these abilities, as we shall see in the next chapter, are critical for success in school, both academically and socially.

LEARNING AND SOCIAL CHALLENGES: HOLDING YOUR SCHOOL-AGE CHILD IN MIND

Every afternoon when seven-year-old Emma's mother, Cara, met her at the bus at the end of their driveway after school, she asked, "How was your day?" As Emma skipped cheerfully down the path to their house, she would invariably say, "It was bad; I had a stomachache." When consulted, her teachers spoke of a bright, happy child who had many friends and was thriving. Multiple doctor visits all concluded that there was nothing physically wrong with Emma.

But the stomachaches were getting worse, and Emma was resisting going to school.

Cara's rational self could see that there was nothing seriously wrong with Emma, yet she was highly distressed by these complaints. "Where does it hurt?" Cara would ask calmly, as she had been advised by many friends and doctors not to make a big deal of Emma's complaints. The idea, she assumed, was that the less attention she paid to the problem, the more likely it was to just go away. But inside she was screaming, "What's wrong with my child?" Not able to let it go, Cara would ask about the pain. This was always followed by Emma's elaborate description of all the social traumas of the day. "Suzy was coloring with Anna and then when Anna wanted to sit with me, Suzy got mad at her and wouldn't talk to her for the rest of the day! Then Anna got mad at me and wouldn't sit with me at lunch!" Cara immediately felt her own level of distress escalate as she tried in vain to help Emma make sense of these school-day trials and tribulations. She felt an intense need to fix all these conflicts, to make them go away. As she offered her daughter suggestions about what do so that everyone would get along, Emma became increasingly annoyed. Often she would say, "Now my stomach feels worse!" Not only was Cara unable to help her manage the conflicts with her friends, but she was also adding to the problem. Yet they were stuck in this daily ritual.

When Cara's husband, Jason, was home to meet Emma, she didn't complain about stomachaches. They concluded it must be something about the way Cara was reacting to Emma that was exacerbating her symptoms. Cara reminisced with Jason about her own experience in school when she was Emma's age. Her parents were going through a divorce, and any kind of conflict put her on edge. She recognized in speaking with Jason that she became so stressed when Emma described her daily social hurts that she was completely unhelpful. Jason, on the other hand, could calmly listen without feeling that he had to fix everything. Once Emma had unloaded all the accumulated tensions of the day on her father, she happily went off to play.

The Art of Listening Calmly

By talking with Jason and with Emma's teachers, Cara came to see that Emma's squabbles with her playmates were normal and developmentally appropriate. She was looking to her mother to help her manage and contain her feelings about these troubles. But Cara felt drawn into the conflicts and reacted to Emma's stories on a physical level. She felt a surge of adrenaline and stress that was way out of proportion to the actual events. Because of her anxiety that something might be wrong with Emma, physically, emotionally, or both, Cara was unable to listen calmly to her and understand what she needed. Instead she would desperately try to convince Emma that everything was fine. This only made Emma's complaints escalate and her stomachaches more frequent.

Once she understood what was happening, Cara felt as if a veil had been lifted. A dramatic transformation took place.

When Emma came home from school, Cara made an effort simply to listen to her tales of woe. Sometimes she had to consciously work to make herself relax, remembering that Emma's complaints were normal for her age and reminding herself to take deep breaths. Cara was then able to hold Emma in mind. She understood that these conflicts among girls are developmentally normal and do not necessarily indicate that something is "wrong." She could empathize with Emma's experience, reflecting the feelings of distress these conflicts with her friends caused her. Cara could help Emma contain her feelings by listening to her story and then moving on with her to another activity. She acknowledged Emma's distress while recognizing it for the minor problem that it was, rather than panicking and reacting as if it were a crisis. Cara began to see where her feelings came from and to separate them from Emma's experience. In doing so she could help her daughter manage the daily frustrations of being a seven-year-old girl. Within weeks the stomachaches subsided almost completely. Perhaps most important, Cara was giving Emma an opportunity to practice managing her own feelings in the ups and downs of her relationships with her friends. Supported by her mother's calm presence, she could stay calm and handle herself in the face of the social roller coaster typical of school-age girls.

In the years leading up to school, a parent, by reflecting on a child's experience in the ways I have described, helps to develop the centers of his brain responsible for reflecting on his own and others' feelings. In the school-age years, these abilities become further developed and consolidated. A child becomes increasingly sophisticated in his ability to empathize with others and understand another person's point of view. These abilities will serve him well with both the academic and social challenges of school.

Emotional Control and Learning

When a child enters school and is still struggling with regulation of his feelings, if he is inflexible and has difficulty taking another person's perspective, the problems he experiences will increase in severity. These problems may occur in the realm of learning, in the realm of social relationships, or both. A child who is flooded with anxiety will have difficulty thinking clearly. Learning and attention both require the ability to regulate emotions. A child who becomes overwhelmed by angry feelings may also have difficulty making friends and may become physically aggressive. Inability to think about feelings leads a child simply to act them out. Children may become impulsive, which literally means to act without thinking. Often children who are identified as bullies are in fact struggling with emotional regulation.

Children who have difficulties learning may have problems with what are known as "executive functions." These include working memory and regulation of attention, two skills that are very important when we pursue goals or solve problems. There is a very close connection in the brain between areas responsible for executive function and those responsible for emotional regulation. One group of researchers in this field describes what they refer to as "cool" executive function, which is related to intelligence. "Hot" executive function, on the other hand, is linked to the ability to think about and monitor emotions. Together, problems with regulation of behavior, emotions, and attention may be labeled as ADHD.

Learning and attention problems in the school setting represent a very complex set of issues and are beyond the scope of this book. For an excellent in-depth discussion of the subject, see *Different Learners* by educational psychologist Jane Healy. My aim in this chapter is to show how learning and attention may be linked with difficulty regulating emotions, and how the way parents react to such difficulties can alleviate or aggravate them. Many children referred to my pediatric practice to be evaluated for ADHD have in fact struggled with emotional regulation for many years.

Regulation of Anxiety and Aggression

Ten-year-old Mindy's parents, Jack and Irene, came to see me, asking if she might have ADHD. In fourth grade she still did not know her times tables. She could read at grade level, but she would forget what she had read almost immediately. She was distracted and unfocused in school. Her parents described her as disorganized, another cardinal feature of ADHD.

When I met with Mindy I was struck by the high level of anxiety she experienced every day at school. Irene had described her messy locker and backpack stuffed with papers as evidence of her disorganization. But when I spoke with Mindy alone about the state of her locker, she explained why she did not take the time to place her things carefully in her locker or backpack. She had an intense fear of missing the bus. Once she had thought her mother was picking her up, and when she realized that she was mistaken, she had run to get the bus but was too late, and the bus left without her. She had to wait in the office while a school secretary called her mother, who arrived a short time later to pick her up. Both Mindy and Irene vividly recalled the incident: Mindy sitting quietly in the office, making every effort to hold it together, and then collapsing in hysterical sobs when her mother finally arrived. Mindy lived in fear that this might happen again.

Mindy had always been a very anxious child. When she was two, she had been home when her house caught on fire. She and her parents had escaped without harm, to her grandparent's house next door, but Irene recalled that Mindy had watched the scene from a window and had cried the whole time. From that day on Mindy needed to know where her mother was at every moment. Once when Mindy was seven, Irene had gone to take the garbage out and Mindy, not knowing where she was, had called 911. There was a strong family history of anxiety. Mindy's mother recalled that she was afraid to sleep in the dark. Mindy's grandmother, her father's mother, suffered from severe panic attacks. However, there was no family history of ADHD. Mindy's parents acknowledged a significant amount of tension in their marriage, and Mindy often witnessed major arguments between them.

Psychological testing revealed no evidence of a learning disability or ADHD. Rather, it was anxiety that was interfering with Mindy's ability to think clearly. At the age of ten Mindy's anxiety had become much more a part of her than it was of three-year-old Cole. Her treatment is more complex. Learning to regulate her anxiety might involve a combination of insight into its cause and cognitive behavior therapy to learn some techniques to manage her distress. I recommended that she have her own individual therapy to address this problem.

But equally important was that her parents recognize and understand the meaning of her "behavior problem." Jack and Irene, at the recommendation of Mindy's teachers, had been thinking of her difficulties as due to possible ADHD. Some teachers had in fact suggested that medication might be helpful.

Jack and Irene saw that Mindy's disorganization and distracted behavior were caused by her feelings of anxiety. They could understand that her anxiety was due to a combination of her genetic vulnerability, the trauma of having witnessed her house burn down, and the ongoing conflict between her parents.

Irene began to connect her own history of anxiety with Mindy's experience and could empathize with her distress. In an effort to help Mindy contain her anxiety, Irene and Jack made clear plans every day for how she would get home from school and enlisted the teacher's help in reassuring her that she would not miss the bus. They also made efforts not to fight in front of Mindy when they realized that their problems were interfering with Mindy's ability to learn.

Mindy had heard the discussion of this possible diagnosis of ADHD. She had heard it from her teachers, from her parents, and in my office. She was enormously relieved that her parents understood why she was having trouble in school. At a follow-up visit when her grades had significantly improved, she told me joyfully that her ADHD had been "cured."

Besides anxiety, anger and aggression may be hard for a child to regulate. These emotions can make social relationships particularly challenging. A child may not have the capacity to reflect on his feelings and then explain in words, "I'm angry that you got ahead of me in line." Instead, he may be flooded with rage, lash out, and hit another child. Thinking back to the neuroscience discussion in chapter two, there is a part of the brain that would in a sense "observe" the feeling of anger and send a message to the lower centers of the brain to turn down the response. But without this self-reflecting ability, the more primitive parts of the brain act unopposed, and a child experiences a fight or flight response. He may be unable to control the impulse to hit the other child. When a child feels threatened in this way, the areas of his brain responsible for rational thought do not work well. A teacher's well-meaning efforts to discuss the problem often lead to escalation of the out-of-control behavior. Many parents have described to me just such a scene, which more often than not results in a child going to the principal's office or being sent home from school. Psychiatrist Bruce Perry has an excellent series of articles on the Scholastic website about aggression and emotional regulation in the school setting, including one titled "Keeping the Cool in School: Promoting Non-Violent Behavior in Children." The articles are written for an audience of teachers, but they may be useful for parents as well.

Bullying behavior is closely linked to difficulty regulating aggression. As we have seen in the preceding chapters, this difficulty may have its origins in early development. Toddlers who need to learn to control their healthy aggressive feelings may grow up in environments in which the adults in their lives are not able to help them with this task.

Assertiveness, generally considered to be a positive quality, actually has a similar meaning but looks different in a two-year-old. Wanting a red truck that another child grabbed out of his hands, but lacking the verbal skills to express intense emotion, a toddler may take the truck and whack the other child on the head. Parents clearly have the responsibility to teach a child that such behavior is unacceptable. But in order to learn to manage his aggression as he grows up, a child needs to know that his feelings are acceptable, but the behavior is not.

If a parent has experienced violence in her past, she may misinterpret a child's normal assertiveness. When he whacks another kid, or hits his mother, she may experience a surge of stress and even rage. These overwhelming feelings do not fit the situation, and they can make it very difficult to see it from her child's two-year-old perspective. Rather than help him control his aggression, she may convey a sense that the feelings are "bad." When a child gets the idea that his feelings are wrong, these feelings don't go away. They just become disconnected from the child's sense of himself. Unable to think about his feelings, he may simply act them out.

Austin had just started first grade when his teachers suggested to his parents, Gary and Jean, that he come see me for an evaluation. He was unable to stand in line and was hitting other children. He had spit at a teacher. Other parents had complained about his "bullying" behavior. Austin's parents described him as "an angel" at home. During our first visit his parents described a very peaceful household and said they were bewildered by his difficult behavior in the school setting. They described very strict limits to any aggressive behavior. Austin was always sweet and loving with his baby sister. His parents were clearly giving him the message that aggressive feelings were bad. In my office, when he played with the dolls, having them hit each other, his mother told him to stop.

The school, as is very common these days, suggested that Austin might have ADHD and implied that he might need medication. Gary and Jean were very upset with the school and canceled a follow-up appointment with me. I did not hear from them again for a year. In second grade Austin's aggressive behavior had become much worse. When his parents made an appointment, I asked that they come without Austin so that they could openly fill me in on all that had happened in the past year. They were furious that Austin had been labeled the class "bully." They felt that any problems in the classroom were always immediately blamed on him.

This time a very different story emerged. Austin's parents had split up. Reluctantly they admitted that the rosy picture they had portrayed a year before was less than accurate. In my office open hostility quickly erupted. When I asked what it might be like for Austin to witness their conflict, at first they turned on me, saying angrily that their relationship had nothing to do with the question of whether Austin had ADHD. But when I suggested that the arguments he witnessed might be causing him some stress, Jean began to cry. She told me about her abusive father. She said that because of her experience growing up, she "hated aggression." Any signs of it had caused her great anxiety. She was much more comfortable with her daughter, who had a gentle, easygoing temperament.

Now we had a very different way to think about Austin's problems in school. The impulsivity the teachers had observed in school and that they had attributed to ADHD, was in fact a result of his inability to think about his feelings. Instead he would simply act out his anger. While he was living in an environment filled with tension and hostility, he had never had the opportunity to learn to manage his own normal aggressive feelings. It was no wonder he lashed out at the other children.

The reasons for Mindy's anxiety and Austin's impulsive behavior were long-standing. Mindy was born with a tendency to be anxious and had then experienced life events that significantly increased her level of anxiety. Austin's difficulties were connected to his mother's own history of abuse and his parents' ongoing marital conflict.

The Developing Brain

But even with such long-standing problems, contemporary neuroscience research gives reason for hope. In *The Brain That Changes Itself*, Norman Doidge, MD, offers an excellent review of the extensive evidence of the brain's *neuroplasticity*. This refers to the brain's ability to form new connections or be "rewired." These new circuits can develop throughout a person's life, though the brain is most "plastic" from birth until the mid-twenties. Jack and Irene, by getting the appropriate support for Mindy, working on their marriage, and holding Mindy in mind during her episodes of anxiety, have the opportunity to "rewire" her brain's response to stress. Austin's parents, due mostly to their own stress and his mother's history of trauma, had difficulty helping Austin manage his aggressive feelings. But armed with an understanding of what the problem is, and with help for themselves to manage their own stress, it is certainly possible for them to work toward "rewiring" Austin's brain. In doing so they will help him learn to manage his aggression even in the complex social politics of school.

But the burden should not fall exclusively on parents' shoulders. It is important for schools to recognize that not all problems with paying attention are due to ADHD. Teachers can be important allies for parents in the task of holding a child in mind, especially in helping parents understand a child's level of development. Certainly it is appropriate for teachers to point parents in the direction of getting help when their child is struggling, but suggesting that children get evaluated for ADHD, as frequently happens, can cause parents, teachers, and clinicians to narrow their thinking before having a full assessment of the reasons a child is having trouble paying attention.

In addition, just as it is important for parents to understand a child's point of view, when children go to school and are behaving in unacceptably aggressive ways, it is again essential to recognize the meaning of the behavior. Simply enforcing "bully-free zones" will not work. Often bullying reflects children's experience of stress and violence at home. Teachers, working together with parents, continue to have an important role to play in helping children think about and manage difficult feelings. Mental health professionals, working with both the child and his parents, by supporting parents' efforts to hold their child in mind, also have the opportunity to move development in a healthy direction.

Secure attachment in early childhood, as we have seen in the preceding chapters, continues to set the stage for success in the school-age years. A number of studies of attachment that follow children from infancy into their twenties offer an excellent demonstration of this connection.

Longitudinal research by Alan Sroufe, PhD, at the University of Minnesota has demonstrated a clear connection between secure attachment and success in the preschool setting. Sroufe and his colleagues have followed a group of more than two hundred children from birth into their twenties. They found that the patterns of attachment in infancy were highly predictive of how a child behaves in the nursery school setting. Bowlby describes Sroufe's findings in *A Secure Base*: "Children who showed a secure pattern with mother at 12 months are likely to be described by nursery school staff as co-operative, popular with other children, resilient, and resourceful." In contrast, those children who were found to show insecure attachment behavior at one year struggled in the preschool setting. Many kept to themselves or showed hostility toward other children. They were more easily frustrated and behaved impulsively. These findings in turn were highly predictive of a child's social relationships in elementary school. Sroufe and his colleagues could most accurately predict success in future peer relationships when they combined measures of attachment in early childhood and peer relationships in preschool.

Sroufe's study looks at the connection between early attachment relationships and peer relationships. Mary Main and her colleagues in the Berkeley Longitudinal Study set out to show that early attachment relationships actually affect the way the mind is structured. Main and her colleagues made use of the research methods I described in chapter four, the Strange Situation and the Adult Attachment Interview, as well as another well-standardized test, the Separation Anxiety Test (SAT). Using these tests, the Berkeley group found a clear association between secure attachment in infancy and children's later cognitive resourcefulness and flexibility of attention and emotions.

The infants who had been found to have insecure attachment were found at both age six and age nineteen to have limited ability in resourceful problem solving. For example, at age six both children rated secure and those rated insecure in infancy were able to describe, as part of the SAT, feelings of distress when presented with a story depicting a child's separation from a parent. The secure children were able to think flexibly about a solution to the problem. The insecure children, on the other hand, were unable to think of a solution. When asked about possible solutions to the problems presented in the pictures in the SAT, they said things like "I don't know," or "nothing." The children with insecure attachment histories, in Main's words, "seemed unable to imagine a useful or constructive strategy for acting on [their] self-admitted feelings."

In summarizing her findings, Main reflects that the children with a secure attachment history have an underlying confidence and calm. Thinking back to the neuroscience, this calm likely reflects the fact that the observing, self-regulating parts of the brain are working. A child can experience intense feelings, whether anxious, fearful, angry, or excited, without being thrown into a state of chaos. When feelings are not regulated, however, the centers of the brain responsible for thinking and problem solving do not work well. In a nervous system that is not well regulated, two different reactions to stress are possible. A child may be what is referred to as "hyperaroused." When the lower centers of the brain are not well regulated by the "observing" brain, the sympathetic nervous system gets activated, and a child may experience a "fight or flight" response, which interferes with the structures of the brain that are important for learning. For example, the hippocampus, responsible for memory, may turn off under stress. The other possibility is that if a child is overwhelmed by feelings, such as may occur with the experience of terror, he may have what is referred to as a "dissociative" experience. The parasympathetic nervous system, not the sympathetic nervous system, is activated. Whereas the sympathetic nervous system is like the accelerator, the parasympathetic nervous system is like the brake. Rather than a fight or flight response, a child simply freezes. In this situation the mind, in a sense, shuts down. When a child is "dysregulated" he may bounce between these two states of "hyper" and "hypo" arousal without being able to comfortably settle in the middle. It is in the middle that a child feels calm. The brain functions well, and a child can learn.

Parents, with the support of teachers and mental health professionals, can, in the words of therapist and teacher Francine Lapides, function as "neuroarchitects." By being attuned to their child's experience and the meaning of his behavior and responding appropriately, they can literally model the brain. They help his brain to stay in that middle zone between hyper and hypo arousal. In that way he can make the best use of his cognitive abilities. Psychologist Pat Ogden refers to this middle zone as the "window of affect tolerance." By thinking about the meaning of behavior and empathizing with a child's feelings, in turn supporting a child's efforts to think about his own feelings, parents can have a positive impact on memory, problem-solving skills, and a child's ability to think clearly and flexibly.

As children make the transition to adolescence and adulthood, their own ability to hold someone in mind, to be fully present with another person, becomes part of their character, part of who they are. This ability is important for all future adult relationships. However, as we shall see in the next chapter, the self-reflection and empathy that have been developing and consolidating over the school-age period may seem to disappear. This phenomenon is in part responsible for the turmoil of the teenage years.

SUPPORTING THE SEARCH FOR IDENTITY: HOLDING YOUR TEENAGER IN MIND

The teenage years have much in common with the melodrama of the toddler years, but on a different scale. Sometimes when I listen to parents describe their struggles with their teenage children, I see in my mind two figures, one struggling to contain another, sometimes bigger than herself, in an unequal battle. But the tantrums of adolescence involve not thrashing arms and legs, but rather words, often cruel and vicious words. Once again Winnicott writes of this stage in a way that I believe can serve to guide a parent through this often-tumultuous period:

> If you do all you can to promote personal growth in your offspring, you will need to be able to deal with startling results. If your children find themselves at all they will not be contented to find anything but the whole of themselves, and that will include the aggression and destructive elements in themselves as well as the elements that can be labeled loving. There will be this long tussle which you will need to survive.

The Work of Adolescence

A teenager's main developmental task is not only to move toward separating from and becoming independent of her parents, but also to consolidate her own individual identity. In his essay "The Eight Ages of Man," child psychoanalyst Erik Erikson describes adolescence as the stage of "Identity vs. Role Confusion": "The sense of ego identity, then, is the accrued confidence that the inner sameness and continuity prepared in the past are matched by the sameness and continuity of one's meaning for others, as evidenced in the tangible promise of a 'career.'" Many teenagers, even if they appear to be thriving, with many friends and excellent school performance, will describe daily struggles with questions such as "Who will I sit with at lunch?" and "Do I look OK?"

The anxiety that goes along with the tasks of separation and identity formation that compose what psychoanalyst Peter Blos calls the "second individuation" (toddlerhood being the first) may decrease a teenager's ability to think about other people's feelings. Her ability to hold others in mind may go offline with stress. It can be bewildering to parents when their child, who was becoming so grown up and sophisticated, suddenly seems transformed into a self-centered, inconsiderate person, oblivious to other people's feelings.

When making decisions, teenagers use the primitive centers of their brains more than they do the areas that are responsible for self-observation. Functional MRI of the brains of teenagers shows that they underuse the medial prefrontal cortex, which as we have seen, plays an important role in regulating emotions. It is not only hormones that impair their thinking. The way their brains work is actually altered. This may also explain the rapid mood swings typical of this stage of development.

Sixteen-year-old Eva and her mother, Pam, had planned to have a nice lunch together. Eva was busy at school and had developed an increasingly serious relationship with her boyfriend, Chris. The intensity of their texting, which began the moment Eva opened her eyes in the morning, and their elaborate efforts to see each other despite their busy schedules, spoke to Pam of young love. Eva and Pam had always been close, and both eagerly anticipated this opportunity to spend a bit of time together over lunch. Things started off well enough. Eva excitedly told her mother about the latest social happenings at school and about a paper she was working on. But then over some little thing, Pam couldn't even remember what it was, Eva had exploded with a burst of venomous rage. "You never think about my feelings," she'd started with, calmly enough. But when Pam tried to get her to explain what she meant, Eva's anger only increased. Vicious insults started flying at her. Caught off guard, Pam found herself becoming defensive.

Their discussion escalated into a shouting match as Pam quickly paid their bill and they left the restaurant. In an effort to get home without being in an accident, Pam stopped talking to Eva, who, she felt, was becoming increasingly irrational in her verbal assaults. She knew from prior experience that engaging with her daughter in a head-to-head battle would only make things worse. Pam's silence only further enraged Eva, and she screamed at her mother, who held tight to the wheel, hands shaking. They made it home and immediately went their separate ways. Pam called her husband. As he was not the recipient of the full intensity of Eva's onslaught, he was able to support his wife and help her to calm down. Eva closed the door to her room and called her boyfriend. Several hours later she emerged from her room. "I'm sorry, Mom," she said. "I've been feeling so much stress trying to balance work and friends and Chris." "I understand you're having a hard time," replied Pam, "but it is not acceptable for you to speak to me the way you did." She explained to Eva that further such outbursts could result in a loss of privileges.

While Pam had been able to navigate the earlier stages of development with Eva, the intensity of feelings directed at her by her teenage daughter was sometimes too much to bear. Yet Pam was doing just what she needed to do, namely withstand the full intensity of her daughter's feelings, both the negative and positive ones, while setting limits on her behavior. Pam's task was to show Eva that she loved and supported her, but would not allow her to destroy her mother.

Eva and Pam had many such scenes over the course of her teenage years. These are most likely to occur at times when a child is confronted with her imminent adulthood, such as becoming involved in a romantic relationship or going off to boarding school or college. The anxiety associated with these experiences and other seemingly minor ones may impair the functioning of the parts of her brain responsible for reflecting upon and regulating strong emotions. A teenager may in fact behave like an overgrown two-year-old. Pam had a solid support system and her own resources to help her manage these frequent and trying confrontations. Setting limits in the face of such behavior, yet showing empathy for the source of the emotional distress, is just as critical at this time as it is during the toddler years. Recognizing that the stage is temporary is essential. If a parent hangs in there through the "long tussle," the observing brain—and with it the ability for empathy and self-reflection—will start working again.

Fourteen-year-old Bennett and his parents, Gordon and Beth, were having frequent confrontations similar to those between Eva and Pam when they came to see me in my pediatric practice. But they did not reach moments of reconciliation.

Gordon and Beth fought frequently about Bennett's difficult behavior. Gordon reported to me that Beth was so upset with her son that she had given her husband the job of finding out if there was something "wrong with Bennett." Bennett was becoming increasingly argumentative and could be sullen and downright nasty. Yet there were times when he was kind and gentle, as he had been as a younger child. His father wanted to know what I could do to "make him be nice all of the time." He had heard that medication was being used to treat cases of "oppositional defiant disorder."

Gordon told me that he grew up in a very rigid household. "We were never allowed to talk back to our parents." I asked him why he thought Bennett might be acting the way he was. As he spoke of his son's growing independence, he realized that Bennett might feel conflicted over losing the close relationship he had shared with his mother and father. Yet while Gordon recognized the importance of Bennett's separation, he refused to accept that his difficult behavior might be a normal part of negotiating this stage of development. In fact he became enraged at my suggestion that some of Bennett's oppositional behavior might even be appropriate, accusing me of giving his son permission to be nasty. I pointed out to Gordon that Bennett was doing well in many other aspects of his life: his grades were excellent, he had several close friends, and he was very involved with several sports. I attempted to show him that this "nasty" behavior was clearly specific to his relationship with his parents and thus must have some meaning. When I resisted the idea of framing Bennett's behavior as some kind of disorder, his parents stopped coming to see me.

A Passionate Ambivalence

While each stage of development has its own challenges for a parent, holding a child through the inevitable rages and passions of adolescence requires an inner calm and strength beyond what the younger stages required. With their increasingly sophisticated thinking skills, teenagers become adept at "pushing your buttons." But ironically, just when a teenager is most actively and aggressively pushing you away, she most needs you to be there.

There is a book for parents of teenagers with the marvelous title *Get Out of My Life, but First Could You Drive Me and Cheryl to the Mall?* This captures the intense ambivalence of adolescence. But a teenager not only needs you to be a chauffeur. She needs you to help her contain and manage strong emotions. Exemplifying the confusing nature of teenagers' emotional states, one patient of mine, a sixteen-year-old girl, told me about overwhelming feelings of anxiety. Yet when I attempted to arrange for a psychiatric consultation to evaluate the severity of her concerns, her reply was, "I don't have time for that—I have to go to cheerleading practice!"

Pam's task with Eva has all of the elements of holding a child in mind that I laid out in the previous chapters. Pam understood that as Eva became close to her boyfriend, in a sense practicing for an intimate adult relationship, she needed to separate from her mother in a way that was painful and difficult. Once Pam could think clearly and was not being assaulted by a screaming child, she understood that the rage directed at her came in part from Eva's sadness over the loss of intimacy with her mother that this healthy new relationship with her boyfriend represented. Eva was overwhelmed by the intensity of feelings, many of which she was likely unaware of, in this transition. Her anxiety decreased her ability to recognize that she was hurting her mother's feelings. Add to this the fact that falling in love inevitably makes a person self-absorbed, and it was no wonder Eva temporarily lost her capacity to see things from her mother's perspective. Eva's ability to reflect on her own and others' feelings was thrown into chaos, and Pam, in turn, needed to work hard to reflect on Eva's experience and not become overwhelmed by her daughter's verbal assaults.

Remembering the passions and turmoil of her own adolescence, Pam could empathize with Eva's feelings. Yet she was also able to set firm limits on Eva's behavior when the abusive language got to be too much. She made it clear to Eva that such behavior was unacceptable and would have consequences. Pam was able to get beyond her own feelings of distress. It helped that she had a strong marriage, with a husband fully present to support her.

Eva, once she had calmed down and wasn't in the throes of rage and anxiety, could recognize that she had hurt her mother's feelings. This was a preview of a relationship between two adults. Eva, by being held in mind throughout her life, is now able to reflect on her mother's experience. This bodes well for her ability to show empathy to the next generation and sets the stage for transmission of secure attachment.

Winnicott offers a hopeful look at the future:

> Your rewards come in the richness that may gradually appear in the personal potential of this or that boy or girl. And if you succeed you must be prepared to be jealous of your children who are getting better opportunities for personal development than you had yourselves. You will feel rewarded if one day your daughter asks you to do some baby-sitting for her, indicating thereby that she thinks you may be able to do this satisfactorily; or if your son wants to be like you in some way, or falls in love with a girl you would have liked yourself, if you had been younger. Rewards come *indirectly*. And of course you know you will not be thanked.

Winnicott's acute insights point out the negative feelings stirred up in parents of adolescents. You may feel jealous of your child, who is the recipient of a depth of understanding that was never shown to you. Such feelings can make the work of being present through "this long tussle" very hard. The parent of a teenager needs a lot of support. Unfortunately, unlike the earlier stages, when there were playgroups, trips to the playground, and parent meetings at school, parents of teenagers are more isolated than parents of younger children. Perhaps Bennett's father did not have the opportunity to have his own experience recognized when he was a teenager and did not now have a chance to see friends struggling with their own children. Bennett's mother was allied with his father in her highly negative view of Bennett's behavior and did not bring in another perspective. This made it difficult for them to hold Bennett's experience in mind in the way he needed.

Important Disruptions

Eva and Pam's story shows a pattern of disruption and subsequent repair, an idea I introduced in chapter one. Both learned a great deal from this interaction, though while it was happening it was hard to experience as anything other than horrible. Eva saw that her mother could survive her rage. She also learned to contain her feelings by having limits set on her behavior. Perhaps most important, both she and Pam had an experience of anger, with an explosive break in their usual close relationship, yet they were able to forgive and move on. Certainly there will be many such disruptions as parent and teenager navigate their way through the jungle of feelings that go along with this "second individuation."

What happens if, as was the case with Bennett and his parents, everything must always be "nice" and there is no room for disruption, if the parents cannot tolerate any "nastiness?" A teenager is left with two choices. She can give up and comply with their wish that she always be nice. If she does this, she may not successfully achieve separation and her own identity and may remain in a way merged with her parents in a regressed manner. Alternatively, she can totally reject her family in an effort to free herself from the restrictive environment that does not make room for any difficult feelings. Clearly neither is a happy outcome.

When parent and child are in the throes of one of these moments of disruption, it is hard to see any benefit. But in fact, in working through these misunderstandings, a teenager acquires a better understanding of her own feelings. The process of disruption and repair actually helps to solidify her emerging sense of her own identity.

When Further Help Is Needed

While much of the drama associated with teenagers is typical and to be expected, symptoms of more serious mental illness may emerge in the adolescent years. Holding a child in mind is just as essential in this situation. Jennifer was a fourteen-year-old whose mother, Maryanne, came alone to my office asking for some strategies to change her daughter's behavior. She said Jennifer seemed to have a hard time seeing the good things in life and needed to "learn to relax." When I met with Jennifer alone, she sat in the corner of the exam room with her coat on and pulled up against her ears. She appeared extremely uncomfortable. As soon as I started talking to her, she became tearful and said that she worries all the time. When I asked if she felt sad, she began to cry, but was clearly making a great effort to hold in her feelings. I asked if her parents knew about these feelings. She said she did not want them to know, that I was not to tell them, and that she was particularly afraid to tell her mother how sad she felt. After speaking a while longer, including asking directly about any suicidal thoughts or intentions, which she denied having, I promised not to share what we had spoken about. I then asked her parents to come in the room.

At first, as Maryanne had at our initial meeting, both parents spoke about wanting to find a technique to help Jennifer "not let things get to her" and "see how good life really is." With time, though, Maryanne began to talk about herself. She said, "It's funny but when you asked about my family history last time I said there was nothing. But I went home and spoke with my brothers and realized that they had suffered from severe depression." Maryanne said she herself had significant depression, but dealt with it by keeping busy and never being alone. She said she was uncomfortable talking about this in front of Jennifer but realized that it was important for her to know. Maryanne then looked at Jennifer and said that perhaps she was feeling sad. I asked Jennifer what she thought of this, and she became tearful again and said, "She's right." I suggested that rather than finding a relaxation technique, Jennifer would need to express and manage these feelings. They accepted a referral for a consultation with a therapist. When I saw them two weeks later, there was a marked transformation in the whole family. Jennifer was beginning to communicate more openly with her parents. She was no longer tearful in school. She had met with a therapist, with whom she appeared to have bonded, and she was scheduled to go once a week. Maryanne was addressing her own struggle with depression.

Jennifer's mother had been unable to see what her daughter was feeling because of her need not to acknowledge those same feelings in herself. Once she began accepting these feelings in herself, she was able to empathize with Jennifer. The transformation brought about by her recognition of Jennifer's feelings shows that although the depression itself was likely of significance in producing Jennifer's symptoms, the fact that her feelings were not recognized by her mother was an equal, if not more important, factor.

When I meet a family for the first time when the child is a teenager, it is not uncommon for parents, like Bennett's father, to describe their teenager in very negative terms, characterizations that are openly discussed in the presence of the child, who has been identified as "difficult." Both parent and child have been worn down by years of struggle. Many of these children are already on medication for ADHD.

Anthony was one such teenager. His mother, Hope, brought him to see me about adjusting his ADHD medication after the pediatrician who had been treating him retired. I encouraged her to meet with me alone, because during our visits with Anthony present she would speak so harshly and critically that it made me uncomfortable. "He's just lazy," she would say. "He's always been impossible." When we met alone, she described a deeply troubled relationship with Anthony since he was an infant. He was a fussy baby who cried easily and did not like to be held. Anthony, now fifteen, was her middle child, and both his older and younger siblings, Hope said, had always been much more easygoing. The children were close in age, and she vividly recalled feeling overwhelmed by Anthony when she became pregnant with her third.

As a toddler he was alternatively clingy and explosive. Hope clearly recalled intense feelings of inadequacy. She described Anthony's sensitivities to touch, taste, and sound and also remembered that she had similar sensory difficulties as a young child. In fact, as we spoke Hope recalled that she had suffered terribly when her own parents were drawn to her older and younger siblings, who were much more easygoing. Taking the time to reflect with me, Hope was startled to find that she had followed the exact same pattern with Anthony. When he was young, Hope did not have an opportunity to reflect on what was happening. Instead, a negative pattern of interaction was set in place. She described to me becoming enraged with Anthony, only to find that his behavior became more difficult. Her marriage was strained, and there were high levels of conflict and tension, all of which were increasingly blamed on this "problem child." Anthony had been on medication for ADHD since he was nine, but Hope revealed to me that she had always questioned the diagnosis, saying, "it's more complicated than that." I worked with Anthony and Hope for a year, meeting with them for a fifty-minute visit every three months. I would ask about the medication, while also talking about other aspects of Anthony's life. I started to meet for half the visit with Anthony alone. In each visit I suggested that talking with someone on a more regular basis would probably be helpful, but they did not follow through. Finally, at the end of one session Hope said to me, "Anthony feels that he would like to talk with a therapist." I referred them to a wonderful colleague who fortunately took their insurance and had time available.

For Anthony, it is likely that the world did not feel like a safe, comfortable place from day one. To make sense of the world and manage his feelings, he needed more help than other children who did not have these biological vulnerabilities. Yet his parents, without the support and space to think about what was happening, fell into scolding and getting irritated with him. Likely at that critical time when Anthony, as a young child, would have been developing the capacity to reflect on his own feelings, his parents were having great difficulty empathizing with his experience. He was not an easy child, and they were preoccupied with managing a busy household. In retrospect, Hope recognized that she could have used someone to help her contain and manage her own experiences raising this challenging child. But she didn't have such help.

If a teenager has never developed a capacity to think about her own and others' feelings, if she has had a very troubled relationship with her parents from very early childhood, she will likely need intensive help. Peter Fonagy and colleagues have developed a form of intensive psychotherapy, Mentalization Based Treatment (MBT). The major aim of MBT is to develop a person's capacity to reflect on her own and other people's feelings. I suspect that Anthony will need this kind of intensive treatment to turn his life in a more positive direction.

My colleague and I met for lunch after Anthony had been in therapy for about two years. She filled me in. While he did need extra help, he was doing better in school. He was developing a better sense of himself and of his interests. He had some close friends. Perhaps most important, his parents, who also met regularly with my colleague, were beginning to express pride in their son. Although occasionally they reverted to old familiar patterns and spoke negatively of him, they could recognize what they were doing and redirect themselves to support him in a healthy way. The unspoken guilt and anger were now out in the open. They understood that the problem was neither in them nor in Anthony. It was in their relationship. They were committed to doing the hard work necessary to heal.

Taking Off from a Secure Base

Eva, Bennett, Jennifer, and Anthony's stories represent the range of difficulties families can encounter as they negotiate the challenging terrain of adolescence. Being that secure base, holding your child's feelings in mind, continues to be an essential part of your relationship as that child herself becomes an adult and goes on to have a family of her own. Bowlby writes about the secure base being important throughout the life cycle:

> The requirement of an attachment figure, a secure personal base, is by no means confined to children, though, because of its urgency during the early years, it is during those years that it is most evident and has been most studied. There are good reasons for believing, however, that the requirement applies also to adolescents and to mature adults as well. In the latter, admittedly, the requirement is commonly less evident, and it probably differs both between the sexes and at different phases of life. For those reasons and also for reasons stemming from the values of western culture, the requirements of adults for a secure base tends often to be overlooked, or even denigrated.

The continued need for a secure base from which to separate is evident in the fact that divorce often affects children the most during adolescence. This issue is poignantly portrayed in the film *The Kids Are Alright*, when the eighteen-year-old daughter, so eager to go off to college and be free of her controlling mother, suddenly looks like a sad, frightened little girl when her parents, in the throes of terrible marital conflict, are preparing to leave her at school.

It is perhaps ironic that much of what we do as parents, from the moment a child is born, helps her to grow up and leave us. This fact lends a level of poignancy and ambivalence to the whole process of parenting. Yet I think every parent would agree that our wish is to raise a child who is, in the words of Bowlby, "self-reliant and bold in his explorations of the world, cooperative with others, and also—a very important point—sympathetic and helpful to others in distress." The works of Winnicott, Bowlby, Fonagy, and all the others I've discussed in this book explain how holding your child's mind in mind in the early years will help develop just these qualities.

Bowlby's thinking converges with Winnicott's concept of the "good-enough mother" when, in the conclusion of his book *Attachment*, he writes that the overarching purpose of a secure attachment relationship, from "cradle to grave," is to give a person the resilience to deal with the inevitable challenges of life:

Thence-forward, provided family relationships continue favorable, not only do these early patterns of thought, feeling and behavior persist, but personality becomes increasingly structured to operate in moderately controlled and resilient ways, and increasingly capable of continuing so despite adverse circumstances. . . . Thereafter on how someone's personality has come to be structured turns his way of responding to subsequent adverse events, among which rejections, separations and losses are some of the most important.

The emergence of the term *helicopter parents* to describe parents who continue to be intimately involved in their children's lives when they leave for college, including reading and correcting papers, points to the trouble we are having as a culture in allowing our children to experience disruptions of any kind. The signs we see that the twenty-something generation is having difficulty separating and leaving home are also perhaps a symptom of our inability to let our children struggle, maybe even experience failure, and in doing so learn and grow from their mistakes.

The "good-enough mother" does not insulate and protect her children from life's struggles. She reflects their experience and contains their distress in a manner appropriate to their level of development. She holds them in mind through the difficult times, from interrupted nursing to the turmoil brought on by the search for identity and everything in between. In doing so she gives her children the tools of empathy, flexibility, and resilience, a secure base from which to become an effective adult.

9

BEYOND MEDICATION

The last decade has seen an explosion of major psychiatric diagnoses in young children and with this an exponential growth in the number of children on psychiatric medications. This is due both to marketing by the pharmaceutical industry and our society's expectation of a quick fix. Managed care has also resulted in limited access to mental health services. This is due to many factors, including poor reimbursement and prohibitively complex administrative costs for private practitioners. Many therapists elect not to be on insurance plans for these reasons, and thus the best care goes only to those who can afford to pay for it. Those few therapists who take insurance, including Medicaid, tend to be overwhelmingly busy. The insurance industry has also created a health care system in which in order to earn a living and cover the cost of the large staff required to manage the administration of a practice accepting a variety of insurance plans, primary care doctors are forced to see more and more patients in less and less time. Prescribing psychiatric medication is a common endpoint of all these social trends.

Raising a generation of children on psychiatric medication in this way will, I believe, have dire consequences. Not only do these medications have significant side effects, but the long-term effects on the developing brain are unknown. When families rely primarily on medication, children do not have the opportunity to develop coping skills to adapt to new situations and frustrations. Equally important, in medicating the symptom away, the underlying issues in relationships are not addressed. Medication can have the effect of silencing everyone.

The Misuse of Medication

Those who advocate use of medication in young children with a range of behavior problems argue that stress hurts the brain and that these medications can protect the brain from this stress. When children and parents feel out of control, when there is sleep deprivation and explosive behavior, both parents and children experience a great deal of stress. It is not surprising that giving a powerful drug that acts on the brain would calm a child down.

But medication is not the only way to reduce stress. As I describe in chapter two, being understood by people who love you also reduces stress at the level of brain biochemistry. Reducing stress and changing the brain in this way is hard work. It requires sustained effort and a lot of support for parents. But the changes are safe and may last a lifetime.

Four-year-old Jeremy could not sit in circle time at preschool. While the other children quietly listened to the teacher, he ran around in circles. He "failed" an evaluation for kindergarten when he could not sit at a desk and follow instructions like the other children. His parents were devastated when the preschool teacher suggested he be evaluated for ADHD. But with careful consideration and sound advice from friends and family, they took another route. Jeremy was among the youngest kids in his class. His parents decided to put him in a different school that was less structured and have him repeat a year of preschool before going off to kindergarten. Jeremy was a sensitive child who was easily overwhelmed in a stimulating environment. They understood his running in circles not as a problem but rather as his way of calming himself down. Perhaps, they reasoned, he just needed time to grow into himself. They proved to be correct. He fit right in at his new school and by the time he entered kindergarten was developmentally right on target. Two recent studies have in fact shown that kids who are the youngest in their class are 60 percent more likely to be diagnosed with ADHD than those who are the oldest. In addition, the youngest children in fifth and eighth grades are nearly twice as likely as their older classmates to regularly use stimulants to treat ADHD. I wonder how many of them would have benefited from a different environment and an extra year of development before tackling the more rigid structure now seen in many kindergarten classrooms.

I am not "against" psychiatric medication, which can in certain circumstances offer significant benefit. Medication may be indicated, particularly in older children, if symptoms are so severe as to impair a child's ability to function. It may calm down the symptoms sufficiently to allow a child to make use of other forms of help. Polarizing the discussion in terms of who is pro-or anti-medication is not useful. My concern is not the use of medication per se, but rather the overreliance on medication to treat complex problems. There are several consequences of particular concern. When the goal is simply to curtail difficult behavior, a child does not learn to recognize the feelings behind the behavior, let alone how to control it himself. In addition, family problems are often set aside in an exclusive focus on managing the child's medication.

For example, a ten-year-old boy diagnosed with ADHD did very well initially on stimulant medication. As he entered adolescence, he began to be argumentative and occasionally oppositional, as was appropriate for his age. His parents, however, saw his behavior as a "symptom" of his ADHD. All family conflict was channeled into discussing his dose of medication. In turn he became increasingly angry, perhaps because his experience was not recognized and his legitimate feelings were attributed to a "disorder."

Many clinicians prescribe psychoactive medication based on a visit with only one parent. Once a father called me to set up an appointment to discuss medication for ADHD. I learned that he was divorced and that the child split time between both parents' homes. I told the father that for ADHD evaluations I preferred to meet with both parents for the initial evaluation. He said he would call me back to set up a time, but never did. Often I will hear one parent say, "His father (mother) is totally against medication." Imagine being a child in such a position. One parent wants you to be on a drug that affects your brain. Your other parent is against it. Your doctor, without even discussing it with your other parent, prescribes it anyway. Yet this kind of situation happens all the time.

I also wonder what it does to a child's sense of self to sit in a room once every three months and listen to a conversation about his behavior and its relation to a pill he takes every day. Often things are said like, "He's just terrible when he misses his dose." Follow-up visits when medications are being prescribed for major psychiatric diagnoses such as ADHD are usually thirty minutes long. Often a child sits and listens to discussions of his behavior in relation to dose and side effects of medications. Visits like this do not offer an opportunity to explore a child's experiences and concerns in any meaningful way. Yet this frequency and duration of visit, and line of questioning, is the standard of care in both pediatrics and child psychiatry and what parents have come to expect. Visits to a psychotherapist for "behavior management" may be recommended in addition to medication.

Again, the focus is usually on making a child behave better, rather than exploring the meaning of behavior. Often there are significant life events contributing to a child's symptoms.

Requiring a full mental health evaluation, including a careful assessment of family relationships, may safeguard against some of these potential negative effects of prescribing medication. In addition, it is essential to offer the opportunity for ongoing discussion with a child, within his family and in the practice where the medication is prescribed, about his diagnosis and issues of importance to him. In particular, talking with a child about his understanding of what the medication is doing and what it means to him to be taking medication for his behavior is very important. Kyle Pruett, MD, a child psychiatrist at the Yale Child Study Center, offers an eloquent discussion of the complex meaning of psychiatric medication to children and families in *Pediatric Psychopharmacology*.

Stories That Need to Be Told

Another serious consequence of overreliance on medication is that it has the effect of silencing experiences and memories that need to be uncovered. The effects of this may not be seen for many years but may persist over a lifetime. Future generations can be affected when significant traumas are not addressed.

In the Academy Award–winning film *Precious*, the main character's transformation comes about largely through her ability to tell the story of her trauma, specifically in the form of writing. She is encouraged in this endeavor by a loving teacher. In *History Beyond Trauma*, two French psychoanalysts argue that symptoms their patients exhibit represent the horrors of war that are not spoken of, sometimes for generations. The patient is relieved of his symptoms when the stories of trauma are finally told, usually in the setting of the relationship between patient and analyst.

These works brought to mind a referral I recently received in my pediatric practice to prescribe medication for a six-year-old boy. The psychological testing report read, "Given these findings relative to attention and working memory, it would be prudent for _____'s parents to share these testing results with their pediatrician regarding a medication trial aimed at mitigating his difficulties with self-regulation and attentional control."

Two years earlier I had seen these parents, Rebecca and John, for a consultation. Rebecca was feeling overwhelmed. Jack would get overstimulated in groups of people. He was becoming increasingly oppositional. They had adopted Jack after taking him in as a foster child when he was three. Prior to this he had lived with his mother, an actively drinking alcoholic. She had physically and emotionally abused him, saying frequently that she wished she'd never had him. His father was in prison and had never been involved in his life.

Rebecca and John wanted some advice about what to do to manage Jack's challenging behavior. I began at that visit to introduce the idea that early trauma can have a significant effect on children's behavior. Important research conducted by Miriam

Steele guided my thinking. She and her colleagues studied children who had all suffered serious adversity, including neglect and both physical and sexual abuse. What was it, she and her colleagues wanted to know, that led to a positive relationship between an adoptive parent and child?

They found that one key factor was the adoptive parent's ability to try to understand the child's behavior as related to his earlier experience. Over twenty-five years of longitudinal child development research have demonstrated what can happen to children who have been hurt by the very person who was supposed to protect them. This paradoxical situation leads to confused and confusing behavior in relationships with people close to them. When children fear the same person they look to for safety at a time when their brains are rapidly growing, this experience affects the biochemistry of the brain. It creates what is referred to as a state of "hyper-arousal." This means that a child has great difficulty regulating emotions and may have an overabundance of stress hormones released in response to what seem like minor events. He does not know how to feel calm and safe.

When parents did consider the meaning of their child's behavior in relation to the child's previous history, when they held their child's experience in mind, they were more likely to describe joy and pleasure in the relationship. On the other hand, when they saw themselves as rescuing the child, without recognition of the continuing impact of previous trauma, their experience of the child's behavior, as Arietta Slade describes in her comments on Steele's research, was "quickly distorted by anger, disappointment and despair."

I wanted to help bring Rebecca and John to this place of understanding. While I did offer some of the advice they were looking for, I also recommended that they engage in therapy for the whole family. I acknowledged that raising a child with a history like Jack's could be extraordinarily difficult. Even with all the love, safety, and security they were giving him, teaching him how to trust and to regulate his feelings, things children usually learn in the first years of life, would be a big challenge for all of them.

Another story of adoption demonstrates the powerful effects of understanding the meaning of a child's behavior even under adverse circumstances. I vividly remember Rachel's "aha" moment. She had brought her six-year old-daughter, Amber, to see me because she was aggressive and defiant. Amber had experienced significant neglect in her first year and had then been shuttled from foster home to foster home before being adopted at age four.

When Amber first came home, she was a terrified child with little language. She immediately began to thrive. But now, at age six, she was wearing the whole family down. Amber would argue about everything, and frequently these arguments turned into physical battles. Rachel was exhausted and discouraged. She wanted my advice about what to do to control Amber's behavior.

The adoption agency gave Amber's new family little information about the effects of early trauma on behavior and development. Thus her parents were bewildered by the fact that the discipline techniques that had been so effective with their biological children failed completely. I wanted to help Rachel to understand the magnitude of the challenge she and her husband faced, while at the same time not discourage her.

On that magical day of the "aha" moment, Rachel was feeling resigned and deflated. We were focusing on some strategies to manage difficult mornings when she began to talk about her biological children. She suddenly recalled a term from the homeschooling philosophy on which they had been raised: "tomato staking." It referred to the way parents stand firm while their developing children twist and turn as they grow up. A parent is always present to guide them in the right direction and does not ever abandon them.

The image was a vivid one: these plump juicy red tomatoes, healthy because of the strong and steady stake that did little more than stand there. But, Rachel realized, Amber did not have this experience in her early years of development. Following this visit, Rachel's approach to Amber changed. She sought out intensive help for Amber. She realized that the whole family needed support in coming to terms with the enormous challenges they faced. Though the work was very hard, the self-blame and guilt from which she had been suffering all but disappeared.

I did not hear from Jack's family for two years, when I received the report suggesting I prescribe medication. They had not followed through on my recommendation for family therapy.

Perhaps the task seemed overwhelming. Stimulant medication will likely be of help to Jack in the short term. Many children who have been traumatized feel much calmer on medication. It may even help them to learn. The problem comes when a child has experienced stressful life events and medication is used instead of, rather than in addition to, therapy. Alleviating symptoms with medication often decreases motivation to do this difficult but important work.

Precious, in the context of a caring relationship with her teacher, was able to tell about her experience. The patients with a history of war trauma similarly had this chance in their relationship with their therapist. Medicating Jack will be only a Bandaid. It may temporarily fix his difficult behavior in school (activities such as massage, martial arts, and horseback riding can also be used to calm his over-reactive nervous system). Underneath, however, will be an open wound that will only begin to heal when he has the opportunity not only to tell his story, but also to have his story heard.

New Labels, New Medications

Recently while cleaning out my office in anticipation of a new job, I discovered that I had unknowingly been witness to a historic moment in child psychiatry. I found a binder from a course I had taken in June 2001 sponsored by Harvard Medical School, "Major Psychiatric Illnesses in Children and Adolescents." Though I did not remember until I looked at my scrawled notes

KEEPING YOUR CHILD IN MIND

in the margins, on Saturday, June 9, 2001, I attended a lecture given by Janet Wosniak titled "Juvenile Bipolar Disorder: An Overlooked Condition in Treatment Resistant Depressed Children." Little did any of us at the lecture know at the time that, largely as a result of Dr. Wosniak and her close colleague Joseph Biederman's, ideas, we would over the next nine years see a fortyfold increase in diagnosis of this "overlooked condition." These children were described as irritable with prolonged, aggressive temper outbursts that she called "affect storms." Some children were as young as three, and over 60 percent were under age twelve.

As this was in a sense a new disease, there were no controlled treatment trials. Wozniak described how she and Biederman reviewed charts of children seen with this constellation of symptoms in a psychopharmacology unit from 1991 to 1995. Patients received a range of psychiatric medications, including tricyclic antidepressants, stimulant medication such as Ritalin, selective serotonin reuptake inhibitors (SSRIs), and mood stabilizers. Wozniak did not mention atypical antipsychotics.

Between 2000 and 2010, four atypical antipsychotics (also known as second-generation antipsychotics)—Seroquel, Zyprexa, Risperdol, and Abilify (clinical trials for a fifth, Geodon, were halted when children in these studies were found to have received overdoses of the drug)—were approved for treatment of pediatric bipolar disorder. So here we have a perfect storm: a "new" disease with no clearly identified treatment and a new type of drug. The number of prescriptions for atypical antipsychotics for children and adolescents doubled to 4.4 million between 2003 and 2006. A recent study done at Columbia University also found that for privately insured children between the ages of two and five, antipsychotic use doubled from 2000 to 2007. Atypical antipsychotics are among the most profitable class of drugs in the United States. Further complicating this story is the fact that Biederman was found to have earned at least $1.6 million in consulting fees from companies that make these drugs, while reporting only $200,000 of this income to his employer, Harvard University. He is currently under investigation for possible violation of federal and university research rules designed to police potential conflicts of interest.

It is not surprising that these powerful drugs, which are also used to control psychotic symptoms in adults, are effective at controlling the explosive behavior associated with what Drs. Wozniak and Biederman labeled as bipolar disorder. But I wonder if this perfect storm may have prevented us from understanding these children in a way that leads to meaningful interventions.

In addition to recognizing the risks of overreliance on medication, it is important to consider the effect of labeling young children with a major psychiatric disorder. In a *New England Journal of Medicine* article with the intriguing title "Pediatric Mental Health Care Dysfunction Disorder?," Gabrielle Carlson, a psychiatrist at SUNY Stonybrook, and her colleagues address the controversy over the new diagnostic label temper dysregulation disorder with dysphoria (TDD). This disorder will appear in the newest version of the American Psychiatric Association

Diagnostic and Statistical Manual of Mental Disorders (DSM), the main psychiatric reference work and source of these labels. The authors of this new version hope to stem the rising tide of prescribing of antipsychotics for young children by offering an alternative diagnostic category that will not necessarily lead to treatment with medication. (Critics of the new diagnostic category worry that it will make normal tantrums into a "disease.") To explain the reasoning behind this new diagnosis, Carlson writes: "No existing DSM diagnosis conveys the appropriate severity and complexity of these children's moods and behaviors: the 'bipolar disorder' label was meant to provide a home for children who were 'diagnostically homeless.'"

But why, I wonder, do young children need to have any label at all? It is not that young children cannot have significant problems for which they and their families need help. As we have seen repeatedly, when children are out of control, both the child and family may suffer terribly. Young children can clearly have disturbances of mood. But what is the purpose of labeling a young child with a major psychiatric disorder?

When parents are struggling with a troubled child, there may be great comfort in having an answer. Many believe that a label points to the correct treatment. But this may not be true. Carlson writes that since the mid-1990s, when a "small but influential group of child psychiatrists" (Wozniak and Biederman) proposed to label children with severe mood dysregulation as "bipolar," the number of children receiving this diagnosis increased fortyfold. "These children, some preschoolers, were primarily treated with mood stabilizers and a new generation of antipsychotic drugs." But, as she acknowledges in her article, the evidence for successful treatment with medications used to treat bipolar disorder in childhood, medications with very serious side effects, is "sparse at best." This fact puts a large hole in the argument that labeling children with this diagnosis leads to appropriate treatment.

Moreover, Carlson points out that "a recent study of large data bases of privately insured individuals showed that most young children given antipsychotic medications did not get psychological support along with it." Only 40 percent had received a mental health assessment, violating the standards of care of the Academy of Child and Adolescent Psychiatry.

Psychiatrist Daniel Carlat has written a book, *Unhinged: The Trouble with Psychiatry*, that explores the disconnection between prescribing of medication and psychotherapy. In his discussion of DSM, he writes, "The tradition of psychological curiosity has been dying a gradual death, and the DSM is part cause, part consequence of this transformation of our profession. These days psychiatrists are less interested in 'why' and more interested in 'what.'" When young children are labeled with a psychiatric disorder, the "why" may not be explored. Treatment may focus primarily on finding the right diagnosis and then the right medication. Yet, as is clear from the many stories I have told in this book, it is the "why" that offers the path to effective treatment.

Yet another argument offered for labeling a young child is that a diagnosis is needed to get insurance coverage for necessary services. Although this is unfortunately true, in my opinion, it is a dangerous example of the tail wagging the dog.

Parents who receive a label of a major psychiatric diagnosis for their child inevitably go through a period of mourning. The child they had is gone and has been replaced by a child with a "disorder." As D. W. Winnicott so wisely observed, a child develops a healthy sense of self when the people who care for him recognize the meaning of his behavior, rather than substituting their own adult meaning. Parents often begin to regard behaviors as "symptoms" of the "disorder." For a very young child whose development is unfolding, his "true self" might be lost in the face of such a frightening label. It is my hope that we can move from an emphasis on diagnosis and labeling to an emphasis on prevention. We need to ask not "what is the disorder?" but rather, "what is the experience of this particular child and family?" and "what can we do to move things in a better direction?"

Supporting Relationships

Fortunately, the shift to medication and diagnostic labeling was not the only development in our understanding of the origins of emotional dysregulation in children. At the same time that our country was experiencing this rapid rise in diagnosis of bipolar disorder in young children, across the ocean in London, Peter Fonagy and his colleagues were providing evidence, based on their research, that, as we have seen, a parent's capacity to reflect upon and understand her child's experience helps that child learn to regulate strong emotions. This research, as this book has shown, offers a completely different paradigm from that offered by the combined forces of diagnostic labels and psychoactive drugs from which to understand what Wozniak called "affect storms." Subsequent research, as I have described, has shown that a child may be born with a genetic vulnerability for emotional dysregulation, but relationships can protect against this vulnerability and increase emotional regulation at the level of gene expression and biochemistry of the brain. The field of infant mental health, with its focus on parent–child relationships, has in fact been growing in parallel to these trends in child psychiatry, exemplified by the publication of Daniel Stern's book on parent–infant psychotherapy, *The Motherhood Constellation*, in 1995, and the works of, among others, Robert Emde, Stanley Greenspan, and Alicia Lieberman. Infant mental health services, unfortunately, are not well covered by third-party payers and are not marketed as widely as prescription drugs. And as we have seen, they require hard work and do not offer the "quick fix" of medication. As such, they are less available as a form of intervention for struggling young children and families.

There are significant forces in our health care system that may make it difficult to support a parent's efforts to reflect upon the meaning of her child's behavior. A story from my practice will illustrate the possible obstacles to care. Five-year-old Max came for an evaluation because his kindergarten teachers were convinced that he had ADHD. They knew little about his life, yet they were pressuring his mother, Alice, to come and see me in the hopes that I would prescribe medication, because his behavior in class was increasingly disruptive. Alice came to the first visit armed with the standard forms, indicating that he had scored in the high range for ADHD.

Though I am part of a pediatric practice in which most visits are ten to twenty minutes in length, I always set aside two fifty-minute visits for evaluation of a child with possible ADHD. I had asked that Max's father come, but as Alice told me her story I saw that this was unlikely to happen. During that first visit, Alice told about her ex-husband, who had been angry and hostile with her in front of Max. She had finally left him when Max was two. Max continued to spend every other weekend with his father, Richard. Alice thought that it was likely that Richard was highly critical of her in front of Max, and she worried about his explosive temper. Alice also told me about her own early history. She described an alcoholic father who was verbally and physically abusive to her mother. She felt an enormous amount of stress as she tried to raise Max on her own, knowing that he might be exposed on a regular basis to an experience similar to her own difficult childhood.

Alice had come to me with a high expectation that I would put Max on medication. However, I suggested that these difficulties she was facing might be making it hard for her to manage Max's challenging behavior at home. In addition, Max's exposure to the ongoing conflict between his parents was likely very stressful for him. I suggested that before considering medication, we take steps to address these significant problems. Alice agreed. Next was the challenge of finding a good therapist who accepted their insurance.

There are very few therapists in our area who accept her type of insurance. Fortunately, a close colleague for whom I have tremendous respect had recently signed on. Her office is also right across the street from mine. So Alice took me up on my recommendation to go for a consultation. While I framed my recommendation in terms of helping Max, when she came for a follow-up visit, she told me how much she had needed that help and that now that she had a place to talk about her feelings, she found herself much more able to handle Max at home. Within a short time, the changes at home began to show up at school, where Max's "distracted" behavior decreased.

Without the luxury of two long appointments, I might never have learned about Alice's story and certainly wouldn't have had a chance to develop the trust necessary for a person to accept a recommendation for mental health care, which is so often stigmatized. If my colleague had not accepted her insurance, I would have had to send Alice to a clinic, where not only is there a cumbersome intake process, but they are so understaffed that even if a person makes a connection with a therapist, visits may be once every two to three weeks, which is inadequate in many situations. Things went well for Alice and Max. However, many times I have uncovered similar stories and things have not gone well. Parents may recognize that they need help for themselves and/or their marriage in order to be able to help their child, only to find that I cannot easily make a referral because of a shortage of qualified therapists who are on the family's insurance plan. The cultural pressure to treat with medication may be too great. Consultation with a child psychiatrist may be of great value in treating a child who is struggling. Unfortunately, I have frequently had the experience of sending a family for a consultation with a child psychiatrist who, after one visit, often with only one parent, gives the child a major psychiatric diagnosis and recommends medication. Many clinicians who prescribe psychoactive medication to children do, in fact, insist that children and families be in therapy. But all too often, due to lack of access to quality care, this good intention proves to be impossible to carry out. In addition, when a child is placed on medication, the motivation to do the harder work of understanding the meaning of behavior may be lost. In the short term, a child may be calmer, and it may seem that the problem is solved. But inevitably, in a few months a family returns, often with a request to increase the dose, as the difficult behaviors emerge anew.

Primary Prevention

Often when I see a family in my office, we can see clearly what is needed, but cannot get from here to there. I believe there is hope, however, in this age of health care reform. The primary care setting offers an ideal opportunity to help parents' efforts to understand their child's feelings, to reflect on the meaning of behavior, and to hold the child's mind in mind, from the very earliest stages of development. A pediatrician has a relationship with a family over time that is usually one of trust and respect and is not associated with the stigma that often accompanies mental health care. This relationship may even begin before the birth of the child. A relationship with a primary care clinician is one of health and normalcy. A referral to a mental health professional, in contrast, implies to parents that there is something "wrong" with a child.

If these ideas are to be applied in a primary care setting on a large scale, however, there would need to be some significant changes in the value we place on primary care. An editorial in the *Boston Globe* addressed the dearth of primary care physicians: "Federal funding for new residency slots should follow reforms that address the underlying reasons— principally money—that lead doctors to choose to specialize." Money is certainly important. But there is another obstacle to attracting primary care doctors that is subtler, though perhaps equally important.

Recently I had the opportunity to teach a group of pediatric interns and residents about contemporary research in child development. As they filtered into the room, I overheard one young doctor wearing scrubs say to another, "I was up in the NICU (neonatal intensive care unit) all night—I'm going to sleep through this one." About halfway through the talk, I asked the group if they had ever been surprised by the things parents tell them in continuity clinic, the primary care experience doctors in training have in which they follow children over a three-year period. I was pleased to see this same doctor's hand shoot up. She spoke about her frustration trying to teach a mother how to control her three-year-old son's increasingly explosive behavior. This young doctor explained that she felt like she was "beating her head against the wall" as the mother of the little boy seemed unable to follow through with anything she said. Then one day, in a way that seemed to her "out of the blue," the mother began to cry. She told the intern about the death of her own mother shortly after her son was born. She admitted to debilitating feelings of depression that made it hard for her at times even to be with her son, much less set limits as the doctor had been prescribing.

This mother's unresolved grief was in the way of her ability to take in this young doctor's "advice." Her trust in the doctor, a result both of the relationship they had developed and the implicit trust people often feel for their pediatrician, had enabled her finally to share these feelings of grief. If this problem had not been uncovered, it is likely that the intern's continued efforts at "giving advice" would have failed.

I asked the doctor to tell us what she had been experiencing while this mother shared her story. She described feeling panicked and inadequate. Not only was she worried about the waiting room full of families who might have to wait longer if she got "stuck" with this grieving mother, but also she didn't know "what to do." The idea that listening to this mother was actually exactly what she needed to do had not occurred to her. She had somehow conveyed to this mother that it was OK to talk about difficult feelings. If doctors do not communicate this interest, it is not because they are not interested. It is because they are under fierce time pressures and fear that they will be inadequate to the task of "solving the problem."

Just as the mother needed to have her experience heard in order to be available for her child, this intern needed the support of her supervisors and colleagues to spend her time this way and to help her manage her feelings. This may have been her first opportunity to share her feelings about this upsetting experience. This way of listening to clinicians in training is referred to as "reflective supervision." Its importance in the education of those on the front lines working with children and families is being increasingly recognized and researched. To hold someone's pain in the way that this intern had to do is not easy. Imagine hearing many stories of trauma and loss over the course of a week. It is very hard to hear these stories without having a place to share the burden. As a matter of self-protection, doctors in training may convey to parents that they do not want to hear concerns that do not appear to be directly related to the child's symptoms. Exhibiting curiosity about the young doctor's experience will support her in her efforts to be curious about the motivations and intentions of parents she sees. She, in turn, may be more likely to encourage these parents to be curious about their children's motivations and the meaning of their behavior.

The Most Important Job in the World

In a lecture given in 1980 titled "Caring for Children," John Bowlby said:

> Successful parenting is a principal key to the mental health of the next generation. . . . In most societies throughout the world these facts have been and still are, taken for granted and the societies organized accordingly. Paradoxically it has taken the world's richest societies to ignore these basic facts. Man and woman power devoted to production of material goods counts as a plus in all our economic indices. Man and woman power devoted to the production of happy, healthy, and self-reliant children in their own homes does not count at all. We have created a topsy turvy world.

Fast forward to the present. Nobel Prize–winning economist James Heckman of the University of Chicago has shown that each dollar devoted to the nurturing of young children can eliminate the need for far greater government spending on remedial education, teenage pregnancy, and prisons. Heckman's research is now guiding the policy of the current administration regarding early intervention for young children.

In this book I hope to have shown that the key to the success of our children lies with their parents' capacity to be fully emotionally present with them; to hold their children's minds in mind. In doing so, they help these growing minds develop the ability to think clearly, learn to control their strong emotions, and engage with the world in a healthy and productive way. If parents are to embrace this challenging yet highly rewarding task, they need to feel valued themselves. Just as a parent needs to hold a child in mind, we as a society need to hold parents in mind.

If we as a country can make a commitment to value both primary care and mental health care, we will have more stories of children like Max, which turn out well. If those who care for children and families on the front lines have the time to develop these relationships, if there is a strong system of mental health care to support families who are struggling and a medical education system that encourages clinicians to listen to parents' stories, we will be well on our way. The image comes to mind of a set of Russian dolls. When the health care system allows the primary care clinician time to listen to the whole of parents' experience and to support their inherent wisdom and intuition, parents are enabled to be fully present with their child. In other words, the system holds the clinician, who holds the parents, who hold the children. Parents in any case must trust their instincts, and if they are struggling, fight to get the kind of help their children need. Policymakers, communities, educators, and healthcare professionals all have a role to play. If resources are allocated for care that supports parents in full proportion to their critical role of raising the next generation, then we as a society could be said to be holding all our children in mind.

NOTES

Chapter One

1   *at my behavioral pediatrics practice*: Some of the stories in this book take place in a typical pediatric exam room. However, when I see a child specifically for a behavioral concern, visits are usually fifty minutes in length, and I use a larger room with comfortable seating, a rug, and a selection of toys

7   *Research at the intersection of attachment theory*:

P. Fonagy, G. Gergely, E. Jurist, and M. Target, *Affect Regulation, Mentalization and the Development of the Self* (New York: Other Press, 2002).

E. Jurist, A. Slade, and S. Bergner, eds., *Mind to Mind: Infant Research, Neuroscience, and Psychoanalysis* (New York: Other Press, 2008).

J. Allen, P. Fonagy, and A. Bateman, eds., *Mentalizing in Clinical Practice* (Washington, D.C./London: American Psychiatric Publishing, 2008).

Fredric Busch, ed., *Mentalization: Theoretical Considerations, Research Findings and Clinical Implications* (New York: The Analytic Press, 2008).

L. Mayes, P. Fonagy, and M. Target, eds., *Developmental Science and Psychoanalysis* (London: Karnac Books, 2007).

9   *it is a crucial human skill with long-term effects*: Arietta Slade, "Parental Reflective Functioning: An Introduction," *Attachment and Human Development* 7, no. 3 (2005): 269–281.

14   *"the holding environment"*: D. W. Winnicott, "The Theory of the Parent-Infant Relationship," in *The Maturational Process and the Facilitating Environment* (New York: International Universities Press, 1965).

14   *the child's "true self"*: D. W. Winnicott, "Ego Distortions in Terms of True and False Self," in *The Maturational Process and the Facilitating Environment*.

14   *as "attachment" behavior*: John Bowlby, *Attachment* (New York: Basic Books, 1982).

15   *between "reflective functioning"*: Mentalization is the broad term used to describe the idea of holding a child's mind in mind; *reflective functioning* is used more specifically in discussing its role in transmission of attachment. P. Fonagy, H. Steele, G. Moran, M. Steele, and A. Higgitt, "The Capacity for Understanding Mental States: The Reflective Self in Parent and Child and Its Significance for Security of Attachment," *Infant Mental Health Journal* 12 (1991): 201–218.

15   *longitudinal studies spanning more than twenty-five years*: K. Grossman, K. Grossman, and E. Waters, eds., *Attachment from Infancy to Adulthood: The Major Longitudinal Studies* (New York/London: Guilford Press, 2005).

16   *field known as "behavioral genetics"*: The references listed in note to page 1 offer material related to both genetics and neurobiology.

16   *neurobiological basis of emotional regulation*: Allan Schore, *Affect Regulation and the Origin of the Self: The Neurobiology of Emotional Development* (New York: Psychology Press, 1994).

Allan Schore, *Affect Regulation and Disorders of the Self* (New York: W. W. Norton & Company, 2003).

Allan Schore, *Affect Regulation and Repair of the Self* (New York: W. W. Norton & Company, 2003).

Daniel Siegel, *The Developing Mind: How Relationships and the Brain Interact to Shape Who We Are* (New York: Guilford Press, 1999).

18   *"I think on the whole if you could choose your parents"*: D. W. Winnicott, *Talking to Parents* (Cambridge, Mass.: Perseus Publishing/Merloyd Lawrence, 1993), 103.

19   *The "Good-Enough Mother"*: D. W. Winnicott, "Ego Distortions in Terms of True and False Self," in *The Maturational Process and the Facilitating Environment* (New York: International Universities Press, 1965).

19   *"Taken for granted here is the good-enough"*: D. W. Winnicott, *Playing and Reality* (London and New York: Routledge Classics, 2005), 187.

20   *Research by psychologist Ed Tronick*: Ed Tronick, *The Neurobehavioral and Social-Emotional Development of Infants and Children* (New York, London: W. W. Norton & Company, 2007).

20   *"the infant internalizes"*: Ibid., 156.

24   *"What to do will flow easily"*: Arietta Slade, "Mentalization as a Frame for Working with Parents in Child Psychotherapy," in *Mind to Mind: Infant Research, Neuroscience, and Psychoanalysis*, ed. E. Jurist, A. Slade, and S. Bergner (New York: Other Press, 2008), 325.

24   *opening words of Dr. Benjamin Spock's*: Benjamin Spock, *Dr. Spock's Baby and Child Care*, 8th ed. (New York: Pocket Books, 2004), 1.

Chapter Two

29   *Contemporary research in neuroscience*: See also references in first note of chapter one.

D. Fosha, D. Siegel, and M. Solomon, eds., *The Healing Power of Emotion: Affective Neuroscience, Development and Clinical Practice* (New York: W. W. Norton & Company, 2009).

Eric Kandel, *In Search of Memory: The Emergence of a New Science of the Mind* (New York: W. W. Norton & Company, 2006).

Allan Schore, *Affect Regulation and the Origin of the Self: The Neurobiology of Emotional Development* (New York: Psychology Press, 1994).

Allan Schore, *Affect Regulation and Disorders of the Self* (New York: W. W. Norton & Company, 2003).

Allan Schore, *Affect Regulation and Repair of the Self* (New York: W. W. Norton & Company, 2003).

Siegel, *Developing Mind.*

30   *Trauma researcher Bessel van der Kolk*: B. van der Kolk, A. McFarlane, and E. Weisaeth. *Traumatic Stress: The Effects of Overwhelming Experience on Mind, Body and Society* (New York: Guilford Press, 2006).

31   *Francine Lapides, in a course*: Francine Lapides, clinical course "Keeping the Brain in Mind," Cape Cod Institute, 2010.

31   Mirror neurons: K. Ensink and L. Mayes, "The Development of Mentalisation in Children from a Theory of Mind Perspective," *Psychoanalytic Inquiry* 30 (2010): 301–337.

36   *"I have referred to the ordinary sensitive mother"*: John Bowlby, *A Secure Base: Parent-Child Attachment and Healthy Human Development* (New York: Basic Books, 1988), 13.

38   *The field grew out of the work of Selma Fraiberg*: S. H. Fraiberg, E. Adelson, et al. "Ghosts in the Nursery: A Psychoanalytic Approach to the Problem of Impaired Mother-Infant Relationships," *Journal of the American Academy of Child and Adolescent Psychiatry* 14 (1975): 387–422.

38   *In the* Handbook of Infant Mental Health: Charles Zeanah, ed., *Handbook of Infant Mental Health, Third Edition* (New York: Guilford Press, 2009), 6.

39 *Psychiatrist Daniel Stern and psychologists*: A. Samaroff, S. McDonough, and K. Rosenblum, eds., *Treating Parent-Infant Relationship Problems* (New York: Guilford Press, 2005), 97–122.

    T. Baradon et al. *The Practice of Psychoanalytic Parent-Infant Psychotherapy: Claiming the Baby* (London and New York: Routledge, 2005).

    Daniel Stern, *The Motherhood Constellation: A Unified View of Parent-Infant Psychotherapy* (New York: Basic Books, 1995).

39 *"good grandmother transference"*: Ibid., 186.

41 *"The relational focus of infant mental health"*: Charles Zeanah and Paula Zeanah, "Infant Mental Health," in *Nurturing Children and Families: Building on the Legacy of T. Berry Brazelton*, ed. B. Lester and J. Sparrow (New York: Wiley-Blackwell, 2010), 234.

Chapter Three

54 *Winnicott described the first weeks*: D. W. Winnicott, *Through Pediatrics to Psychoanalysis* (New York: Basic Books, 1975), 300–305.

    D. W. Winnicott, *Winnicott on the Child* (Cambridge, Mass.: Perseus Publishing/Merloyd Lawrence, 2002).

54 *Winnicott writes: "It will be observed that"*: Winnicott, *Winnicott on the Child*, 18.

55 *Melanie Klein, a major influence on Winnicott's thinking*: Robert F. Rodman, *Winnicott* (Cambridge, Mass.: Perseus Publishing/Merloyd Lawrence, 2003), 251.

57 *Adam Phillips elaborates on this idea*: Adam Phillips, *Winnicott* (Cambridge, Mass.: Harvard University Press, 1988), 128.

60 *"Does he have colic?"*: T. B. Brazelton, *Touchpoints* (Cambridge, Mass.: Da Capo Press/Merloyd Lawrence, 2006), 231–237.

62 *Winnicott describes this way of being*: D. W. Winnicott, "The Theory of the Parent-Infant Relationship," in *The Maturational Process and the Facilitating Environment* (New York: International Universities Press, 1965).

    D. W. Winnicott, "Ego Distortions in Terms of True and False Self," Ibid.

64 *Babies like Anna also experience difficulty with*: T. B. Brazelton and J. K. Nugent, *Neonatal Behavioral Assessment Scale* (London: Mac Keith Press, 1995).

67 *When a parent is struggling with depression*: L. Murray and P. Cooper, eds., *Postpartum Depression and Child Development* (New York/London: Guilford Press, 1997).

71 *Then the need for this exact attunement lessens*: D. W. Winnicott, *Playing and Reality* (London and New York: Routledge Classics, 2005), 14.

Chapter Four

75 *"For a person to know that an attachment figure is available"*: John Bowlby, *A Secure Base: Parent-Child Attachment and Healthy Human Development* (New York: Basic Books, 1988), 27.

76 *"A young child's experience of an encouraging"*: Bowlby, *Attachment* (New York: Basic Books, 1982), 378.

77 *Ainsworth first became interested in understanding*: Ibid., 299–340.

80 *Mary Main, a psychologist at the University of California–Berkeley*: Mary Main, "The Organized Categories of Infant, Child, and Adult Attachment: Flexible vs. Inflexible Attention Under Attachment Related Stress," *Journal of the American Psychoanalytic Association* 48, no. 4 (2000): 1056–96;

82   *Main also added a fourth category to Ainsworth's original three*: E. Hesse and M. Main, "Disorganized Infant, Child, and Adult Attachment," *Journal of the American Psychoanalytic Association* 48, no. 4 (2000): 1097–1127.

82   *Contemporary research by Elizabeth Meins*: E. Meins, C. Fernyhough, E. Fradley, and M. Tuckey, "Rethinking Maternal Sensitivity: Mothers' Comments on Infants' Mental Processes Predict Security of Attachment at 12 Months," *Journal of Child Psychology and Psychiatry* 42, no. 5 (2001): 637–648.

90   *Winnicott's concept of the "transitional object"*: D. W. Winnicott, *Through Pediatrics to Psychoanalysis* (New York: Basic Books, 1975), 229–242.

95   *A number of good parenting books*: T. Berry Brazelton, *Sleep—the Brazelton Way* (Cambridge, Mass.: DaCapo/Merloyd Lawrence, 2003).

       Richard Ferber, *Solve Your Child's Sleep Problem* (New York: Simon & Schuster, 1986).

Chapter Five

98   *"What distinguishes healthy individuals"*: M. Steele and H. Steele, "Understanding and Resolving Emotional Conflict: The London Parent Child Project," in *Attachment from Infancy to Adulthood: The Major Longitudinal Studies*, ed. K. Grossman, K. Grossman, and E. Waters (New York/London: Guilford Press, 2005), 143.

100   *In addition to taste and smell*: Winnie Dunn, *Living Sensationally: Understanding Your Senses* (London and Philadelphia: Jessica Kingsley Publishers, 2008).

       Winnie Dunn, "A Sensory Processing Approach to Supporting Infant-Caregiver Relationships," in *Treating Parent-Infant Relationship Problems*, ed. A. Samaroff, S. McDonough, and K. Rosenblum (New York: Guilford Press, 2005).

       Pratibha Reebye and Aileen Stalker, *Understanding Regulation Disorders of Sensory Processing in Children: Management Strategies for Parents and Professionals* (London and Philadelphia: Jessica Kingsley Publishers, 2008).

100   *Contemporary research in a field known as "behavioral epigenetics"*: There has recently been an explosion of literature on this subject. The following two articles, as well as the one below by Champagne and Curley, offer a good overview of the subject.

       Michael Meaney, "Epigenetics and the Biological Definition of Gene x Environment Interactions," *Child Development* 81, no. 1 (2010): 41–79.

       F. A. Champagne, "Epigenetic Mechanisms and the Transgenerational Effects of Maternal Care," *Frontiers in Neuroendocrinology* 29, no. 3 (2008): 386–397.

101   *Much of the evidence for gene–environment interactions*: David Reiss, "The Interplay Between Genotypes and Family Relationships: Reframing Concepts of Development and Prevention," *Current Directions in Psychological Science* 14, no. 3 (2005): 139–143.

102   *To illustrate how this works*: Stephen Suomi, "How Gene-environment Interactions Can Influence the Development of Emotional Regulation in Rhesus Monkeys," in *Biopsychosocial Regulatory Processes in the Development of Childhood Behavior Problems*, ed. S. Olsen and A. Sameroff (Cambridge, England: Cambridge University Press, 2009).

104   *Similar to the gene Suomi studied*: A. Caspi, A. R. Hariri, A. Holmes, R. Uher, and T. E. Moffitt, "Genetic Sensitivity to the Environment: The Case of the Serotonin Transporter Gene and Its Implications for Studying Complex Diseases and Traits," *American Journal of Psychiatry* 167, no. 5 (2010): 509–527.

104   *"Although these examples of interactions between genotypes"*: F. A. Champagne and J. P. Curley, "How Social Experiences Influence the Brain," *Current Opinion in Neurobiology* 15, no. 6 (December 2005): 706.

107   *The research of Peter Fonagy and his colleagues*: A. Slade, J. Grienenberger, E. Bernbach, D. Levy,and A. Locker, "Maternal Reflective Functioning, Attachment, and the Transmission Gap: A Preliminary Study,"*Attachment & Human Development* 7, no. 3 (September 2005): 283–298.

107   *Fonagy and his colleagues termed this ability*: As mentioned in chapter one notes, mentalization is actually the broader term used to describe the idea of holding a child's mind in mind and "reflective functioning" is used more specifically in discussing its role in transmission of attachment.

108   *Miriam Steele and her colleagues*: J. Hodges, M. Steele, S. Hillman, K. Henderson, and J. Kaniuk, "Changes in Attachment Representations Over the First Year of Adoptive Placement: Narratives of Maltreated Children," *Clinical Child Psychology and Psychiatry* 8, no. 3 (2003): 351–367.

   M. Steele, J. Hodges, J. Kaniuk, S. Hillman, and K. Henderson, "Attachment Representations and Adoption: Associations Between Maternal States of Mind and Emotion Narratives in Previously Maltreated Children," *Journal of Child Psychotherapy* 29, no. 2 (2003): 187–205.

108   *In the early 1990s a group of researchers*: P. Fonagy, M. Steele, G. Moran, H. Steele, and A. Higgitt, "The Capacity for Understanding Mental States: The Reflective Self in Parent and Child and Its Significance for Security of Attachment," *Infant Mental Health Journal* 12 (1991): 201–218.

   P. Fonagy, M. Steele, G. Moran, H. Steele, and A. Higgitt, "Measuring Ghosts in the Nursery: An Empirical Study of the Relation Between Parents' Mental Representations of Childhood Experiences and their *Infants' Security of Attachment*," Journal of the American Psychoanalytic Association 41 (1993): 957–989.

110   *"the speaker's awareness of emotional and motivational"*: Busch, *Mentalization: Theoretical Considerations, Research Findings and Clinical Implications* (New York: The Analytic Press, 2008), 139.

110   *Arietta Slade took Fonagy's idea of reflective functioning*: A. Slade, "Parental Reflective Functioning: An Introduction," *Attachment & Human Development* 7, no. 3 (2005): 269–281.

Chapter Six

128   *The extent to which families talk about feelings*: K. Ensink and L. Mayes, "The Development of Mentalisation in Children from a Theory of Mind Perspective," *Psychoanalytic Inquiry* 30 (2010): 301–337.

129   *as "theory of mind"*: P. Fonagy, G. Gergely, E. Jurist, and M. Target, *Affect Regulation, Mentalization and the Development of the Self* (New York: Other Press, 2002), 24.

Chapter Seven

150   *refer to as "cool" executive function*: Ensink and Mayes, "The Development of Mentalisation in Children from a Theory of Mind Perspective," *Psychoanalytic Inquiry* 30 (2010): 307.

150   *For an excellent in-depth discussion of the subject:* Jane Healy, *Different Learners: Identifying, Preventing, and Treating Your Child's Learning Problems* (New York: Simon & Schuster, 2010).

154   *Psychiatrist Bruce Perry has:* See http://teacher.scholastic.com/ professional/bruceperry/index.htm.

157   *In The Brain That Changes Itself:* Norman Doidge, *The Brain That Changes Itself: Stories of Personal Triumph from the Frontiers of Brain Science* (New York: Viking Penguin, 2007).

159   *Longitudinal research by Alan Sroufe:* A. Sroufe, B. Egeland, E. Carlson, and A. Collins, "Placing Early Attachment Experiences in Context: The Minnisota Longitudinal Study," in *Attachment from Infancy to Adulthood: The Major Longitudinal Studies,* ed. K. Grossman, K. Grossman, and E. Waters (New York/London: Guilford Press, 2005).

159   *Bowlby describes Sroufe's findings:* Bowlby, *A Secure Base: Parent-Child Attachment and Healthy Human Development* (New York: Basic Books, 1988), 127.

159   *Mary Main and her colleagues in the Berkeley Longitudinal Study:* M. Main, E. Hesse, and N. Kaplan, "Predictability of Attachment Behavior and Representational Processes at 1, 6, and 19 Years of Age," in *Attachment from Infancy to Adulthood,* ed. Grossman, Grossman, and Waters.

161   *therapist and teacher Francine Lapides:* Lapides, clinical course "Keeping the Brain in Mind," Cape Cod Institute, 2010. D. Siegel Fosha, and M. Soloman (New York: W. W. Norton & Company, 2009), 204–231.

162   *"window of affect tolerance":* P. Ogden, "Emotion, Mindfulness, and Movement: Expanding the Regulatory Boundaries of the Widow of Affect Tolerance," in *The Healing Power of Emotion: Affective Neuroscience, Development, and Clinical Practice,* ed. D. Siegel Fosha, and M. Soloman (New York: W. W. Norton & Company, 2009), 204–231.

Chapter Eight

163   *Winnicott writes of this stage:* D. W. Winnicott, *Playing and Reality* (London and New York: Routledge Classics, 2005), 193.

164   *In his essay "The Eight Ages of Man":* E. Erikson, *Childhood and Society* (New York: W. W. Norton & Company, 1950, reissued 1993), 261.

165   *what psychoanalyst Peter Blos calls:* Peter Blos, "The Second Individuation Process of Adolescence," *Journal of the American Psychoanalytic Association* 22 (1967): 162–186.

165   *teenagers use the primitive centers:* Sarah-Jayne Blakemore, "The Social Brain in Adolescence," *Nature Reviews Neuroscience* 9 (2008): 267–277.

169   *a book for parents of teenagers:* Anthony Wolf, *Get Out of My Life, but First Could You Drive Me and Cheryl to the Mall?* (New York: Farrar, Straus & Giroux, 2002).

171   *Winnicott offers a hopeful look:* Winnicott, *Playing and Reality* (London and New York: Routledge Classics, 2005), 193–194.

178   *Mentalization-Based Treatment:* J. Allen and P. Fonagy, *The Handbook of Mentalization-Based Treatment* (West Sussex, England: John Wiley & Sons Ltd., 2006).

179   *"The requirement of an attachment figure":* John Bowlby, *The Making and Breaking of Affectional Bonds* (London and New York: Routledge Classics, 2005), 125.

180   *"self-reliant and bold in his explorations":* Bowlby, *A Secure Base: Parent-Child Attachment and Healthy Human Development* (New York: Basic Books, 1988), 82.

180   *"Thence-forward, provided family relationships":* Bowlby, *Attachment* (New York: Basic Books, 1982), 378.

Chapter Nine

184   *Those who advocate use of medication*: In her book, Warner offers this perspective, based on her research primarily within the discipline of child psychiatry. J. Warner, *We've Got Issues: Children and Parents in the Age of Medication* (London: Penguin Books, 2010).

185   *kids who are the youngest in their class*: W. Evans, M. Morrill, and S. Parente, "Measuring Inappropriate Medical Diagnosis and Treatment in Survey Data: The Case of ADHD among School Age Children," *Journal of Health Economics* 29, no. 5 (2010): 657–673.
   T. Elder, "The Importance of Relative Standards in ADHD Diagnosis: Evidence Based on Exact Birth Dates," *Journal of Health Economics* 29 (2010): 641–656.

188   *what it means to him to be taking medication*: K. Pruett, V. Shashank, and A. Martin, "Thinking about Prescribing: The Psychology of Psycopharmacology," eds. A. Martin, L. Scahill, and C. Kratochvil, in *Pediatric Psychopharmacology* (New York: Oxford University Press, 2011), 422–434.

189   *In* History Beyond Trauma: Françoise Davoine and Jean-Max Gaudilliere, *History Beyond Trauma* (New York: Other Press, 2004).

189   *Important research conducted by Miriam Steele*: M. Steele et al., "In the Best Interests of the Late Placed Child: A Report from the Attachment Representations and Adoption Outcome Study," in *Developmental Science and Psychoanalysis*, ed. L. Mayes, P. Fonagy, and M. Target (London: Karnac Books, 2007).

190   *experience of child's behavior*: A. Slade, "In the Best Interests of the Late Placed Child," commentary in *Developmental Science and Psychoanalysis*, ed. L. Mayes, P. Fonagy, and M. Target (London: Karnac Books, 2007), 188.

193   *activities such as massage, martial arts, and horseback riding*: Bruce Perry, "Applying Principles of Neurodevelopment to Clinical Work with Maltreated and Traumatized Children," in *Working with Traumatized Youth in Child Welfare*, ed. N. B. Webb (New York: Guilford Press, 2006).

195   *A recent study done at Columbia University*: M. Olfson, S. Crystal, C. Huang, and T. Gerhard, "Trends in Antipsychotic Drug Use by Very Young, Privately Insured Children," *Journal of the American Academy of Child and Adolescent Psychiatry* 49, no. 1 (2010): 3–6.

195   *In a* New England Journal of Medicine *article*: E. Parens, J. Johnston, and G. Carlson, "Pediatric Mental Health Care Dysfunction Disorder?" *New England Journal of Medicine* 362 (2010): 1853–1855.

197   *Psychiatrist Daniel Carlat has written a book*: Daniel Carlat, *Unhinged: The Trouble with Psychiatry—A Doctor's Revelations About a Profession in Crisis* (New York: Free Press, 2010), 45.

199   *Daniel Stern's book*: Daniel Stern, *The Motherhood Constellation: A Unified View of Parent-Infant Psychotherapy* (New York: Basic Books, 1995).

199   *Robert Emde, Stanley Greenspan, and Alicia Lieberman*: R. Emde, *Revealing the Inner Worlds of Young Children* (New York: Oxford University Press, 2003).
   S. Greenspan, *Building Healthy Minds* (Cambridge, Mass.: Da Capo Press/Merloyd Lawrence, 2000).
   A. Samaroff, S. McDonough, and K. Rosenblum, eds., *Treating Parent-Infant Relationship Problems* (New York: Guilford Press, 2005), 97–122.

203   *An editorial in the* Boston Globe: "Dearth of Primary Care Docs Boils Down to Money," *The Boston Globe*, January 18, 2010.

205   *This way of listening to clinicians in training:* "Putting Reflective Supervision into Practice," *Journal of Zero to Three: National Center for Infants, Toddlers, and Families* 31, no. 2 (November 2010): 22–29.

206   *In a lecture given in 1980:* Bowlby, *A Secure Base: Parent-Child Attachment and Healthy Human Development* (New York: Basic Books, 1988), 2.

206   *Nobel Prize–winning economist James Heckman:* James Heckman, "Schools, Skills and Synapses," *Economic Inquiry* 46, no. 3 (2008): 289.

USEFUL WEBSITES

American Academy of Pediatrics:
www.aap.org

Baby TALK:
www.babytalk.org

The Bernard L. Pacella, MD, Parent Child Center:
www.theparentchildcenter.org

Brazelton Touchpoints Center:
www.touchpoints.org

Bright Futures:
www.brightfutures.org

Infant Massage USA:
www.infantmassage.org

Ounce of Prevention:
www.ounceofprevention.org

Postpartum Support International:
www.postpartum.net

Society of Developmental and Behavioral Pediatrics:
www.sdbp.org

World Association for Infant Mental Health:
www.waimh.org

Zero to Three
National Centers for
Infants, Toddlers and Families:
www.zerotothree.org

INDEX

INDEX

PHOTO CREDITS

ABOUT THE AUTHOR

Claudia M. Gold, MD, has practiced general and behavioral pediatrics for over twenty years, and has a long-standing interest in addressing the mental health needs of children in a preventive model. She is a graduate of the scholar's program of the Berkshire Psychoanalytic Institute and of the University of Massachusetts, Boston, Infant-Parent Mental Health Post-Graduate Certificate Program. She currently practices behavioral pediatrics in Great Barrington, Massachusetts. She has written a series of columns about children's mental health for the *Boston Globe* and writes regularly for her blog Child in Mind (www.claudiamgoldmd .blogspot.com).

Dr. Gold lives in Egremont, Massachusetts, with her husband and children.